HAUNTED
OCALA
NATIONAL FOREST

CHRISTOPHER BALZANO

Haunted
America

Published by Haunted America
A Division of The History Press
Charleston, SC
www.historypress.com

Unless otherwise noted, all images are courtesy of the author's collection.

First published 2022

Manufactured in the United States

ISBN 9781467148665

Library of Congress Control Number: 2022933415

Notice: The information in this book is true and complete to the best of our knowledge. It is offered without guarantee on the part of the author or The History Press. The author and The History Press disclaim all liability in connection with the use of this book.

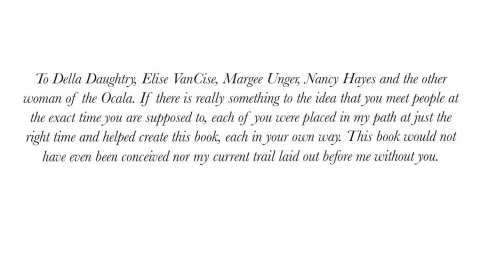

To Della Daughtry, Elise VanCise, Margee Unger, Nancy Hayes and the other woman of the Ocala. If there is really something to the idea that you meet people at the exact time you are supposed to, each of you were placed in my path at just the right time and helped create this book, each in your own way. This book would not have even been conceived nor my current trail laid out before me without you.

CONTENTS

ACKNOWLEDGEMENTS

This book has been a combination of research and discussion with people who offered their stories and personal experiences to help build the folklore up tale by tale and moment by moment. I want to extend a thanks to everyone who crafted this story with their time, including all those who asked to not give their real or full names. Thank you to Kerrie Marie Cherry, Heather Whiteman, Nancy Hayes, Taylor Hoffman, Kimberly Lahr, Hailey Madison Bailey, Logan Jones and Samantha Mae Simpson-Brooks. A special thanks to Lee Ehrlich for his stories and advice. I also cannot thank Della Daughtry enough, even if most of our Pemberton Ferry material didn't make it into this book. She was a constant sounding board and source of support. I also need to give all the love I have to Elise and Triston VanCise, Margee Unger and Jonathan Dolce for asking me to visit their library and igniting this entire project.

A good researcher should always read more than they write, and this book would not have been possible without the writers who gave me ideas and allowed me to steal from them, including Mark Muncy, Charlie Carlson and David Goudsward. I also leaned heavily on the interviews and written words of journalists Dave Schlenker and Rick Allen and turned to the writers of BackPackerVerse for starting off parts of my journey with these haunted legends.

I could not have done this without the support of my family, including my parents and my sister Laureen Caron. As always, Jeff Belanger was the voice in my head telling me to get back to work when I needed to and not to take myself so seriously when I was blocked. A special thanks to those who continued to push me, especially Amanda Collins, whose words always kept me on the path. My kids allow me to take time away from them just long enough to get some work done, and they often came with me when I went to check out places. I could not have written about and tripped some of these locations without Natalie Crist and Deanna Mulhern, who helped me research, find and explore them.

1
THE OCALA SYNDROME

I 'm not really sure if this has anything to do with ghosts or anything like that, but it most certainly does," Kerrie says when she talks about her time in the shadows of the Ocala National Forest. She has lived in Ocklawaha her whole life. It's the kind of unincorporated community you find in Central Florida where the name changes depending on what people are trying to direct you to. Some maps list it as the ghost town of Electra, a clear distinction anyone from Ocklawaha is quick to make but that no one else cares about. That's the name of the cemetery that has more than a few odd stories about it. Others might call it strictly Marion County. The same issue comes up when trying to track down exactly where Panasoffkee might be in Sumter County or the abandoned town of Rosewood in Lake County. There's something about the shifting nature and the forgotten and unspoken history of the towns around the forest that breeds this geographical sleight of hand.

Now twenty-three, Kerrie remembers there always being something creepy about where she lived and the woods that surrounded it. "I always feel like something is watching me. I always look behind the shower curtain when I use the bathroom. When I was about seven, my neighbor came over and did a ghost hunt. She used dowsing rods. She had me come over to her house and drink this tea that tasted like flowers." She tells this story as she rattles off moments of weirdness the way someone tells you a story about a person so you understand who they are before telling you the story they really want to tell you. The problem is, the background information only

A welcoming sign to a not-so-welcoming place.

connects in her mind because she is trying to make sense of each tale as part of a bigger experience.

Recently, for example, something happened she could not explain away. "I'm not really sure if this has anything to do with ghosts or anything like that, but it most certainly does." One night, she and her sister saw weird lights outside, as if someone with a flashlight was trying to steal something on the property. They watched for a while, and then the light went out. As she looked out the window, an eerie face formed in the window she was looking out of, blurry, staring at her with no mouth and no eyes. A male friend came over to stay the rest of the night with them. "It was daybreak, and we saw this heavyset woman with a hunchback come up the hill. She had a black thing in her hand." Her male friend confronted the woman, and Kerrie overheard the old woman say, "I'm the only one." He returned and said she was going up to try to get some gas, which was odd, as there was nothing up the road she was taking. A little while later, a bald man stepped out of the woods and walked angrily in the same direction as the woman.

You wait for the connection, but it's there for her as she tells it.

Kerrie and her sister walked around the house, trying to make sense of what happened that night, and Kerrie saw the strange lights again. "My sister didn't see them, but there were three white and pink lights. They were tiny and went in a circular motion and then up. I didn't know what to think, but I could just feel like they were magical." They also noticed there were traces of burnt plants or tree branches in the yard. Her niece started to call out to them when they noticed another person in the yard she thought was one of her other male friends, but it wasn't. The man seemed to vanish. It was around this time that she also saw the head of a young girl, who they originally mistook for one of their daughters' friends, apparently floating without a body above the shed. This vision also disappeared. Her niece had also seen the young girl. If all of this sounds confusing, it is an example of what hearing a story is often like when people talk of the Ocala. It feels like a ramble, like trying to lay it all out on the table to see if it makes sense when viewed from above.

"I'm not really sure if this has anything to do with ghosts or anything like that, but it most certainly does." That is the kind of thing you hear when you ask people if anything odd has ever happened to them in the Ocala. When Kerrie tells her story, she sounds like so many others I talked to when I started to follow up on the oddness I sensed in the area. Details that seemed unimportant at the time make sense but do nothing to help comprehend what happened. Sentences start and are then stopped, because a detail that occurred earlier in the tale has to be told so that the next part of the story makes sense. Or maybe it doesn't help. In these stories, humans get confused with specters, odd lights become cigarette tips and maybe a person was there, but they don't remember it anymore. You can't ask them to jump to the end or press them for details, because, like Kerrie, they tell their story with the passion of someone who has struggled to process something beyond them. Memories are mixed with half explanations and are expressed in fragments.

A dream about something reveals what a moment might have meant, only to have the person telling you about it second-guess which part of it was a dream and which part might have actually happened. It can be frustrating when you are trying to get the story straight, unless you come to appreciate something residents have known for a while.

Living near the Ocala National Forest means strange things are going to happen, and it is better to let them come and go than to try to fit them in an easy box.

That is what researching the area is like. Founded in 1908, the Ocala covers more than six hundred square miles and is the southernmost national forest in the country and the second in terms of size. Those are the stats you can find on any website that touches on the park, but the real story is something you understand only by going there and talking to the people. It is a place of great beauty and magical springs, but also a dark place that crosses paths with cults and gangs and missing-person cases. People grow up spending some of the best days of their lives stepping off the paths in the woods, but they never know exactly where they were when it happened. It has been the site of movie and television shoots and has inspired poetry and music. It is a place where ghostly folklore and haunted history are part of the everyday narrative of a body of water or a stretch of trees or an abandoned cemetery of only a few broken and unremembered headstones. Everyone has a story to tell, but when they tell it, it is almost as if you have stepped into a conversation that started before you began to listen, because the geography is so common and held so dear that they assume you know it.

Here's another story that tells volumes about the Ocala. I posted in a local online group asking for anything odd that people had experienced. The feedback was overwhelming, something I had not experienced in almost thirty years as a researcher into the unknown. One man contacted me privately and told me to watch the post at 10:30 a.m. He had something to tell me and did not want to say it over the phone or have a digital record of it having been said. He made me promise I would not take a screenshot or try in any way to save what he wrote. He would allow it to remain online for five minutes and then delete it forever. I checked the posting at 10:30. It was a warning about the nonparanormal element within the forest, something I had already started to follow up on. He told me to stop looking into that angle of the forest. Write the book, but do not pursue this aspect of the cult activity there. At 10:34 a.m., the posting was gone, but through other sources I was able to confirm some of what he had told me. Less than a day later, his profile had been deleted from the social media platform.

One of the many dark places just off the beaten path.

I knew I could not tell the whole story of the forest without at least talking about the reputation of the people who find their way there and the way the locals view them. When someone goes missing anywhere in the state, it is always in the back of people's minds that they'll end up somehow connected to the forest. There's twelve-year-old Dorothy Scofield, missing since 1776, and Troy Burress in 1990. People still search for what happened to people like Robert Snowberger, who walked into the forest in 2019 and has not been seen since. The list goes on and on, including body after body that has not been identified. But these cases cannot be given the time each deserves. Instead, when you ask about the weirdness of the woods, people rattle off these cases in almost the same breath as they talk about tales of ghosts and unexplained animals, as if they are all interwoven when it comes to the Ocala.

And talk will always come back to the Rainbow People. The Rainbow Family is part of a larger, informal group whose members have been meeting in select areas throughout the country since the early 1970s, including the Ocala. They are generally law-abiding people who come, celebrate and move on, but the dark draw of the forest and the weather in Florida have encouraged them to stay past their usual winter gatherings. The saying goes that locals know not to buy things, especially hygiene products, during the winter months in the towns near the Ocala when the Rainbow People are known to be around, because the products could be used. It may be an unfair assessment, but the mysticism of the group is enough to make people uneasy, and many believe that other, more lawless elements are working within the group or pretending to be members. Gangs, Satanists and dangerous cults have all been mentioned in the same breath as the group. They get blamed for everything from break-ins and car thefts to abductions, drug trafficking and murders. When someone sees something they can't explain in the woods, they often point to the Rainbow People, especially those who never leave and those who they believe only pose as members of the group. They are the Boogeyman among the trees. Everyone seems to know someone who has had a run-in with them or with someone they assumed was part of the group, and they always recite the story as if there is a cloud of smoke around the experience. They talk of being chased, of seeing people in robes with candles and of plates and forks hanging from trees in a scene straight out of *The Blair Witch Project*.

It's not just the forest. The towns surrounding the woods have the same odd energy and the same types of stories to tell. Places like Astor and Deland easily blend with others farther away like Brooksville and Sanford and even Daytona. The forest gives way to the Green Swamp, and people just shrug their shoulders and talk about them as if they are one and the same. People in some towns almost an hour away consider themselves part of the Ocala and talk about the events that happen to them as being a side effect of their proximity to it. They will begin by saying how strange the woods are and then tell you about something that happened down the street. Again, you just have to listen and nod and take it all in, because at some point, you see, they are all suffering from the same condition, something I call Ocala Syndrome. Like Kerrie, it's all connected in their minds, linked through time and different locations by a central villain with its eyes wide open and staring at them in the middle of it all.

Early on in my paranormal research career, I focused on an area of New England known as the Bridgewater Triangle and wrote the book *Dark Woods: Cult, Crime, and the Paranormal in the Freetown State Forest*. That began with a question: Could the same negative energy that caused so much paranormal activity also be the reason the area had so many cults and odd crime? I thought this book would be much the same, until I began to peel the layers of the onion. In Massachusetts, the forest was like a magnet, drawing in people and spirits and feeding on them like a vampire before choosing its next victim to attract. In the Ocala, people are not drawn in. Instead, they are infected and affected. The activity would happen even if no one was there to see it, like the proverbial tree falling in the woods that may or may not make a sound. They are living in the shadow of the Ocala, but they see it as part of the package. They begin by saying they have something odd to tell you, but by the time they are finished, they have convinced you that it's not that odd, given where it takes place.

So that makes this an odd ghost book, and you should know going in that it probably can't be read like a typical one. I will offer you no evidence. As someone who now specializes in haunted folklore, my work is not grounded in whether something is real or not but rather that people think it is. They spread their tales with certainty, even in the light of facts that contradict their truth. There are plenty of those kinds of stories, but the Ocala forced me to go one step further. It is not a matter of Kerrie's personal story being completely true or all made up. It doesn't work like that here. One story leads to another, which leads to another, and I have tried to capture that narrative style with this book. It's not meant to convince the reader of a truth but to offer context for what people have experienced and the anecdotes they have come to accept as true.

Read it as if you are leaning in, trying to make someone feel better by showing them you care about what they say.

Then maybe when you're done, you can make sense of it. If so, let me know, because the darkness of the Ocala still confuses me.

2

SLIPS AND SHIFTS

In November 2018, I made my way to an area of Florida known as Hog Island to legend trip the story of a swamp witch who was said to be terrorizing people staying at the Hog Island Campground in the Withlacoochee State Forest. It was a pretty straightforward tale that I firmly believed is nothing more than an urban legend. For years, people have reported a dark figure cackling outside of their tents and campers. They hear screams coming from right in front of them, but no one is there. She has been known to tear into shelters and bang on doors and disappear into the night. People walking around the park, built around a swamp—little more than wet ground during the dry season and an overflowing creek when the rains come—see what looks like a woman in a cloak or a large coat who vanishes when she goes around a tree. Others have even reported seeing a figure looking like a thick shadow even during the day, walking across a pond that looks suspiciously like a fairy or witch's circle, glowing an eerie green with algae.

Some say it is the inspiration for *The Blair Witch Project*, created by film students at nearby University of Central Florida. Others claim the witch story is a cover for a possible lynching that took place and was referred to in a local paper. Either way, the stories of weird happenings persist there and had hit my radar. What I didn't know at the time was that we were less than one mile from a spot on the nearby Withlacoochee River that is considered the deadliest place in Florida. I wasn't aware yet that the Dade Massacre had happened basically down the road. I had not fully explored the idea that

One location in the Ocala known for dark figures and "shifting."

there was something unusual in the Ocala and the places connected to it. I was just looking for a swamp witch and planning on using it to record an episode of my show about the fear of the outsider.

When I arrived, my cohost and I took some pictures near the sign at the entrance but then were drawn to an area of the path where the black of the intense heat of a controlled burn made the trees in the distance creep up to form what looked like two hands coming together in an arched entrance. We started that way but were intercepted by a ranger who asked why we were walking around. We talked for a while, and the ranger outright denied having ever heard of a witch story. (He then went on to tell us that his grandmother had been a white witch who had to fight other darker witches in the area.) But the ranger then directed us to the path and encouraged us to stay on it. Twenty minutes later, wading through prickers hanging over our trail and not feeling the ticks attaching themselves to our jeans, we stopped in our tracks. There was a single vine off the path in the swampy woods, swaying like someone was swinging it back and forth. We left the path and made our way to it, and a few steps away, close to those claws we had originally been drawn to, was a thick oak. In that tree, so old and worn it looked almost like part of the bark itself, was a noose snaking its way down. It was the link to the legend we were looking for. We photographed it. We videotaped it. A week later, we passed on the information, including details on how to find it, to author Mark Muncy, who was covering the story for his book *Creepy Florida*. It wasn't there for him that day. I have been back to the location several times since then and have helped several legend trippers try to spot it for themselves. Nothing.

The noose had shifted. It was there for us in the moment, telling us its story, and then was gone.

It was not the first time I had heard of such a thing while looking into ghostly folklore, but it was an idea I would hear multiple times as I looked into the Ocala. Hunters who know the woods like the back of their hand find themselves lost and unable to get out. Hikers, marking places off on GPS devices as they discover little gems on the trails, go back to find them gone, only to be there two weeks later, unmoved. Four-wheelers making their way through well-traveled trails they've ridden for a decade find themselves inexplicably separated from their friends. For as long as anyone can remember, things in the area have shifted. Time has been lost with no explanation.

People can find a reason for a ghost. Even if it's scary. They discover that someone died on their property, and they connect it to what they experienced. Unexplained animals like thunderbirds and Skunk Apes can be chalked up to misidentification or a belief that these cryptids exist. Time slips are a different story. They are the unknown within the unknown, and there is nothing that can be held on to other than theories. The most common leans toward abductions by aliens, something the Ocala is known for, although these are rarely reported to happen during the day. There are some who believe missing time and shifted geography have something to do with the Rainbow People or another, more nefarious, cult within the forest using drugs or even witchcraft to make odd things happen. In the forest, people point to a more concrete cause. People just don't know it the way they think they do. Nature changes from week to week, and when you're in the thick of it, things can seem similar because everything in the woods looks the same.

Then there is the outlier, the explanation that carries too much weight and comes with too many questions. It may, however, explain much of the weirdness people report in the Ocala. The whole area might be the victim of a vortex or a wrinkle in reality. It's a theory that can't be proven except by the symptoms of the problem. Whether it is a crease that allows people to see other dimensions or another reality, this controversial idea has been used to explain large areas with a concentration of supernatural and paranormal events. It explains why Skunk Apes are seen by someone and then seem to disappear. It allows people to understand how a graveyard they visit on Thursday is gone when they try to find it on Sunday.

The first time I was near the Ocala was during a library visit to Astor to speak about haunted legends, not knowing that the people of Astor know all too well about haunted legends. As I stretched my legs after my long car ride, I decided to take some promotional pictures. Although it was almost noon, every shot looks like we were approaching dusk. It was not overcast. The sun was shining brightly, and the day was already almost too hot for anyone to be outside. Reality was sunny, but we could not make the pictures come out that way. Even sound waves were affected. The library, originally built on a swamp, is surrounded by trees and a road lined with buildings. Yet our voices echoed when we tried to talk to each other outside, something I also observed a few years later when I returned for another event the library was holding and again when they asked me to come investigate the activity there. An unexplained force was interfering.

Jennifer might have experienced the same thing. She grew up in Eustis but now lives in North Carolina, partly because she hated all of the spooky things that happened to her growing up. One involved a cemetery down the road from her that would only appear every so often. "I didn't like to explore in the woods, because we all grow up hearing these stories. I'm not sure if they are supposed to be a warning or just the stories all people tell about their town. It's part of living there." Jennifer, whose parents moved away, leaving her little reason to return, says she loved to read and play in her yard as a child but stayed close to the house. One day, she wandered into the trees

A spot known for a disappearing cemetery.

just beyond her safety zone. "There was no noise, I felt something calling me. Not really, but in my head." She followed the voices and came upon a small cemetery with about ten headstones.

"The trees were thick, but it was like noon. There was almost no light, like it was almost sunset or something. There was a little boy who looked a lot like my brother with flowers in his hand looking down at one of the graves. I was about to say something, like yell at my little brother for being out there, when a woman appeared as well. They didn't see me there. The boy put the flowers in front of one of the graves, and they both just walked into the woods."

She ran home and found her brother in the living room watching television. She kept the whole thing to herself, but a week later, she felt drawn back. She took the same route and walked for almost an hour but could not find the graves. "They were right in the woods, right there. But they were gone." She went back several times, but each time she retraced her steps, she came up empty, until one trip when she was fifteen.

"The only times I ever went back there was to look for the cemetery. I'd get scared and not want to even think about it, but then something would tell me to try again. Not like a voice in my head. Like when you know you left something on or forgot to lock the door and you need to go and check. I went back with a camera, determined to find it again and prove I wasn't crazy. Ten minutes and I was there. Years nothing, and then ten minutes. Same graves, but the light was really bright; like too bright. There was no one there or spooky voices telling me to go there." She walked around the area for half an hour, taking pictures and trying to read the headstones. She did see the name Griggs several times. She took pictures. "Old school camera, the kind where you had to get the film developed. I couldn't find the film later, so I have no idea if they even came out."

In the years since, she has tried to research who the Griggses might be. "There are a dozen or so cemeteries near the Ocala called Griggs Cemetery. I've had old friends visit them and take pictures. Half the time they can't find them, and when they do, none of them look like mine. It's just a weird thing I can't explain, but I can't forget it."

It doesn't end with the odd shifting. Sometimes, time itself moves and people experience something that may have happened at another time or in another dimension. Take the Saturday morning that David went down the path near the Tobacco Patch Trail near the Ocklawaha River. He and two of his friends had spent hours on the road on their four-wheelers, taking advantage of the miles and miles of official road and the endless trails just off the main way. The three of them stopped for a moment to talk about heading back home for the day. David followed them back, all of them traveling in a straight line. "The day was over. If you're into riding, you know the way back is boring. You just want to get back." His mind wandered a bit as he drove over the well-known path, but then he saw something odd on the side of the road. Two adults and a child were a little into the woods, dancing. He turned his attention back to the road, and his two friends were gone. "I stopped and watched them for a few seconds. My rig is pretty loud, and they didn't notice it at all. I shut off the engine. They were dancing, but there was no music." David says he wanted to approach them, but there was a "foggy light" around them that unnerved him. He started his four-wheeler again and turned to get one last look. "Gone. Just gone." He says the words slowly when he retells the story, although he never really tells the story to people. He noticed the light had changed dramatically, and when he arrived back home after a journey that should have lasted less than thirty minutes, more than three hours had passed. "My friends just assumed I had turned off and decided to stay. We did that sometimes. When I asked them, they said they didn't even see I wasn't with them until they were almost back at their houses."

Sometimes the shift of the forest can go the other way, drawing people in. Nancy had never been to the Ocala National Forest and, because of her experience, has no desire to go again. She now has the benefit of being three thousand miles away and more than forty-five years removed from her experience. The distance doesn't always help. "I get goosebumps still talking about it, mainly because of the unknown aspect of it." She doesn't understand what happened to her and her friends, and she also gets confused by the why. More than anything, she is still struck by the way it felt to be in the forest when she remembers it more than four decades later.

It started like an average night for her. She was seventeen at the time, and her older sister had a small son. The three of them had gone shopping and then went over to her friend Scott's house to do a little drinking and maybe smoke a little pot later in the night. Scott lived on Siesta Key in Sarasota, about a three-hour drive from the forest. They put the food away and put the baby to sleep. "We all got our drinks and were going to roll joints. But nobody had done it yet." Nancy recalls going into the living room and then nothing.

Four hours later, she was woken up by her sister touching her face, trying to stir her. The first thing Nancy noticed was that she was outside and that the baby was next to her in his car seat. As she tried to gain her bearings, she came to see that she was on a path surrounded by darkness and trees. "I had no idea where I was. None of us did. It was terrifying and fascinating." They spent a few minutes talking about where they were and what had happened, but no one had an answer. "Usually you can rationalize things, but not this." They followed the trail they were on, trying to find anything that was familiar or that pointed to where they were. It was not just that they had been instantly transported someplace they did not recognize; there was an odd energy in the air that Nancy could feel.

"The whole place was just weird. I felt like I was walking through electricity. I felt it all the way until we got to the city at the edge of the forest." She can't fully explain it now, but she could feel that energy through her whole body and was unsettled by the way it seemed to be running through her. To her, it was not a positive energy, the kind she now feels being in the woods where she lives in Oregon, but something darker. It was not until they reached a restaurant and went inside to call someone to get them that they realized they had woken up in the Ocala and had just walked into the town of Ocala. They sat silently outside, no one talking about what had just happened. "We didn't talk about it because you don't even believe it yourself."

That's the way it was for years. She and Scott never mentioned it again, and she and her sister only hesitantly talked about it a few times before her sister passed. Nancy admits they were a bit wild before that night, but after that, everything changed. "We were kids before that, but then afterwards we were not." Scott became a born-again Christian immediately after. She and her sister settled down their partying. They all moved on with their lives, but it was always there in the back of Nancy's mind. She has had unexplained experiences her whole life and feels connected to the wilderness and thick wooded areas, but she never wants to experience what she did that night. "I don't think you could pay me enough. I don't want to feel that again. You can't make sense out of nonsense, and that's what this was."

3

GHOST LIGHTS OF THE OCALA

G o on the internet or social media sites looking for ghosts and you'll see balls of light called "orbs." They are the bread and butter for people looking for evidence that spirits exist, and paranormal investigators and lovers of all things spooky cling to them as sacred. One of the hardest aspects when dealing with the paranormal is meeting people who show you their ghost pictures and having to tell them there are too many natural reasons for these lights to appear. It could be dust, bugs, the reflection of the flash or a shiny surface distorted by perspective and wishful thinking. Some images truly can't be explained, but usually the person walks away disappointed, partially still believing they have the missing link.

Then there are the ghost lights. No matter what people tell you, they are harder to explain away. These are solid balls of light seen in real time and in three dimensions. People observe them with the naked eye hovering or darting back and forth. Skeptics will talk of ignited gas or headlights from cars breaking through little patches in the trees or flashlights or campfires misidentified. There is something to these explanations, but at times it makes what people witness even more physical. Whether it's a phantom light seen swinging down a railroad track when no one is there or balls of yellow and blue light dancing with each other on an abandoned road, people run those explanations through their filters before they share the event. They want to make sense of something when they have run out of logical reasons. Often, there are other strange things that happen and maybe a backstory they heard from a friend or relative or read online, making the moment come alive and make sense. Other times, it's just a moment in time for them. Talk to someone about the weirdness in Ocala, and eventually they will tell you a story about a ghost light.

Lee Ehrlich has seen just about everything in his decades looking into the paranormal. The owner of GhostPro out of Lee County, Ehrlich has made a name for himself through his underwater expeditions and evidence-based approach to the paranormal. He is familiar with every landscape the state has to offer, and there is not much that makes him scratch his head anymore—except maybe the Ocala. He has been out there many times, and each time he comes away convinced its supernatural complexion is unique, especially in the summer. "It all has something to do with the energy that the summer brings. It's the heat. There's lightning in the sky and things are just buzzing. As soon as the forest starts to come alive, the paranormal activity comes alive. Whatever it is that makes things animate reinvigorates the paranormal, like reconstituting the dead."

Della Daughtry's representation of the "Vespers" seen at a cemetery outside the Ocala.

Of all the stories he has of the forest, one thing has been a constant. "Every single time I've been there with a team, I've seen glowing balls of light. The biggest ones have been the size of a Frisbee. The smallest have been the size of a golf ball." Sometimes when his team has been out there, he has seen what looks like car lights among the nearby trees, but their distance from any road or trail big enough to accommodate a vehicle makes that nearly impossible. As someone who has spent time in forests and looking into ghosts, he can tell they are not torches or flashlights. "When you approach them, they'll just float off into the sky. They illuminate trees as they pass by, like they have a glow inside of them." Other times the lights seem as if someone is holding a lantern, but there is no one there. "You go near there [where the lights are] and it just fades away. They don't just fly off so fast that you don't know what you saw. They take their time. They're not in a rush."

The most famous of the ghost lights in Central Florida are easily the Oviedo Lights, also known as the Chuluota Lights. While most orbs are seen in haunted locations associated with other ghostly activity, in Oviedo, the lights are the star, and for decades they were the most popular attraction in

Central Florida you didn't need to pay for. People would get into their cars and make their way to Snowhill Road, or Route 13, and plant themselves near the bridge that goes over the Econlockhatchee River and wait for the show. Once the visitors snuggled themselves in, multiple balls of light would entertain them, flying through the air, passing over cars and dancing with each other. The ghosts' attitudes came out in the way they moved and in their multiple colors. Not all of the stories associated with them were harmless. They could be fatal, especially for anyone looking to get in the back seat with that special someone at the location. If they caught you, your soul became part of the show.

If you can come up with any popular ghostly backstory for why lights appear in the sky, it's been said and believed about Snowhill Road. The most popular involves a soldier coming back from war to find that the woman he loves has married another man. In his grief, he commits suicide at the bridge. His spirit comes back as punishment for his sin and to scare lovers who use the area as a place to engage in car-based actives. It doesn't end there, though. Like many spots where there are multiple accidents, the ghosts are of those who have crashed and died nearby. Then there is the ghost of a Native American killed on the road. The spirit is forced to walk back and forth between the site of his demise and the mound the settlers disturbed in Oviedo. A woman was once in a carriage accident and lost her children near the bridge. She now roams the fields looking for her dead family, who appears as lights in the sky. Don't forget the soul of the Boy Scout who died in the woods during a camping trip. The lights are the other scouts' flashlights looking for the boy. He is never found, and the lights replay themselves until they can find him. Or maybe the orbs are the souls of those who have come to the bridge looking for a fun night of sky watching, only to be killed by the Oviedo Lights themselves and forced to join their dancing.

Pick and choose the backstory that appeals to you.

In the 1950s and '60s, legend tripping the lights was the thing to do on a boring Saturday night. Friends and families hopped in cars to watch them. Couples used them as an excuse to make out in back seats. There was nothing more popular than to travel to the spot, turn off your lights and share your theories on their origins with other people out there that night. The legend tripping was so infamous that students from nearby Florida Technical University, which would become the University of Central Florida, got involved. The school's paper would not only publish articles about lights (even debating whether the lights were dangerous to the students) but also post calendar events sponsored by the university's different clubs to visit the

A roadside view of the Oviedo Lights.

phenomena: On Tuesday, the Art Club will be leading a group of people to see the Oviedo Lights. On Saturday, the Key Club will be offering a bus to the lights as part of its yearly fundraising. The physics department even officially offered to evaluate any evidence gathered to try to determine what the lights might be.

It was all fun and games until the accident in 1963. Seventeen-year-old Norbert Hyman was hit by another car near the bridge and died. Either one or both of the cars had turned off their lights to catch a glimpse of the ghosts. Police tightened up security at the site, but in the end, Hyman became just another part of the lore. Going to see the Oviedo Lights has faded in popularity in recent decades, but the activity comes and goes in waves. Visiting the site is now most popular in the summer months and whenever the lights are featured in a new book, a new documentary is made or a YouTube video about them goes viral. The more attention they are given, the more activity there is.

The reason for the lights at Silver Springs State Park is also a sign of when people have discovered their story, changing their characters and plot with every generation. Once the most popular attraction in the state, the park has changed through the years, and the folklore about why the ghosts are there has always been twisted to match. For years, the park, which was once the shooting location for the *Creature of the Black Lagoon* and *Tarzan* movies, drew people with its glass-bottom boats, which traveled through the clear blue water, allowing passengers to observe the exotic plant and animal life below. As the boats moved, the captains would tell the history of the park and the tale of Claire Douglass and Bernice Mayo. Claire was the son of a rich cotton farmer who employed Bernice. When the two fell in love, Claire's father sent him away. Bernice eventually gave way to her grief, died and was brought to rest in an area of the water known as the Bridal Chamber. Her body was swallowed up by the spring itself as the water sucked her down. When Claire arrived later and heard of her death, he rowed out and jumped into the water. Bernice's hand, still wearing the Douglass family bracelet her love had given her, reached through the water to him, and he was also consumed by the spring.

If you have a hard time believing that these lovers are the reason there are unexplained lights in the water, try to explain why people still see them. There is no swamp gas to be ignited under the water. If it feels like a better argument, you can just claim it is glowing vegetation. Maybe it's a coincidence, then, that the same lights are seen in other places in the park, including at the shops and restaurants. Employees talk about how the orbs look like they are dancing at the new pavilion built for weddings and functions. Then there are the ones seen in the thick flora all around the park. Those can be explained away by the wild monkeys and other wildlife. Something reflects off their retinas, and you have an unexplained phenomenon.

The legend of what the lights are, especially those seen at the Bridal Chamber, changed as the park evolved and became more popular. As the Seminole Village was built in the 1930s, Bernice and Claire were replaced by Tululah and Navarro. The story is essentially the same, though, with their tribes wanting them to stay apart. Tululah dies and is swallowed up by the

Silver Springs, where the ghost lights of lovers are seen on the water.

spring, and Navarro eventually dives in to join her. Then there is the story of Ocklawaha and Winona, which also gains popularity at this time. Again, we have the story of rival tribes and forbidden love, but in this one, the lovers escape and make their way to Silver Springs, only to be found. Rather than be caught, they jump to their deaths.

None of this can be proven or backed up, and if you look too closely at the stories, they fall apart at basic levels. For example, the angry fathers are always leaders who can't be proven ever existed. The stories are so close in their narratives that they obviously borrow from one another. Then there is the fact that no cliff exists near Silver Springs for tormented lovers to jump from. Instead, these are great stories to tell on a boat trip to add some spice, something to give it an even more exotic appeal. Boat captains, especially ones who have been there longer, will tell you they don't tell those stories anymore. "We were told not to," says one old-timer. "When they sell this place, the new people always have their own ideas. I guess maybe people don't want to hear them anymore anyway." He knows of them, even remembers telling them years ago, but now he keeps them to himself. They do not even call the Bridal Chamber by the same name. It is now the Abyss. "'Course, that doesn't mean there aren't still those lights."

His words are echoed by several of the employees, many of whom can recite personal experiences and secondhand stories when asked. "At night here. That's scary. I try not to work late," says one younger employee. "The guards here at night, they are the ones with the stories of the lights. They all see them. In the morning, right before sunrise, this place is eerie. Those guys at night, they are used to it. They say it's like the ghosts are walking around all night." One guard went on to say that he has never seen them but has heard the stories. There has never been anything evil or malicious about them, but he finds excuses to not work there at night.

Not every ghost light is part of an amusement park or inspires generations to legend trip. Most experiences are much quieter and have no mythology attached to them. Take Hailey's experience. When she was a teenager, she was driving with her mother and stopped as a train made its way across the road. "I remember looking out my window and just midway above us was a big ball of green and yellow light just hovering there. I shook my mom and she looked and saw it as well." They remained there for several minutes as the train passed and then followed the train down the tracks. That moment has stayed with her, as has what happened after. "As soon as we got up home, I drew what we saw. My mom commented that it looked identical to what she had seen. I put it on the fridge. The next morning at breakfast, I noticed it was gone." No one in her family had moved the picture, and it was never seen again, even after they bought a new refrigerator years later and moved the old one, although Hailey admits watching it being moved and remembering how the picture had gone missing.

Other stories offer a little inspiration on top of the mystery. Issac was deep in the woods and experienced one of those famous Ocala turnarounds. Although he had been riding his ATV on the trails for years, he found himself lost and losing the sun. He was only seventeen at the time and was getting anxious as he looked down at his gas gauge. "Then this light was there. It was

The view near the Abyss, which people used to refer to as the Bridal Chamber.

green and the size of a baseball. And it was floating there like two feet off the ground." He was sure it was not another vehicle, because he had turned his off and there was no sound as it moved down one of the paths, stopped and then moved a few more feet before stopping again. "Something told me to follow it, so I started down that path. I've seen lights in the forest, but not like this. Usually they are in the sky and maybe it's a fire or something. This one was almost like playing with me." He continued to stay a few yards behind the ball of light as it picked up speed and made several turns. Eventually, he came across a marker he knew and noticed the light was gone. "I've never told anyone this, which is messed up. Everyone has a story like this, but I never told my friends." The reason is odd. While most people would assume something had helped him that afternoon, Issac looks at it the opposite way. He believes the light was the ghost of someone from one of the lost settlements or even a Native American who had been disturbed somehow. The spirit did not help him when he got lost, but something intentionally turned him around or changed the forest so he could have the experience.

Those are the kinds of ideas only a place like the Ocala can inspire.

4

GHOSTLY LEGENDS AND ODD WHISPERS FROM FORT KING

Fort King in Ocala, Florida, has a paranormal identity crisis. It both reflects the oddness people feel in the rest of the city and offers a possible reason for the unexplained things that happen there. Outsiders tell a beautiful if not tragic story of a love to rationalize the odd fog they say rolls in sometimes in the early winter and the vanishing figures that always accompany it. The people who work at the historic site and the people in the surrounding neighborhood tell a darker story, told in much quieter tones, about its bloody history and the stain left behind, which they describe as a curse. It infects the area and makes everything in the town a bit off, as if the people today are paying the price for sins of generations long past. Just ask those in the middle of the storm, those who interact with the phantoms and the unexplained moments. They'll tell you that all the stories are true, not just because they have experienced something or someone they know has, but because one of ghost stories means the other ones make sense, too.

Tourists are told about the American soldier and his beautiful Seminole maiden. Her people had used the spring behind the fort. They had settled in the Ocala area because the water was pure and was known to heal the heart and body, and the spring was the purest source. Even their dead were buried nearby to take advantage of its power after death. It was pretty much left alone by the soldiers at Fort King, not because they did not need to have their hearts and bodies healed, but because it was just far enough in the woods to be dangerous. The Second Seminole War had shifted the base from being a

Haunted Fort King.

buffer between the two sides to a full military necessity. Things were getting bad, and the soldiers were in the middle of it. Some even argued that the war started there. What had once been a natural balance of neighbors became a case of dividing the woods between what was safe and what was not.

One soldier would often find reason to wander back. Since the first day he saw her gathering water, he had been bewitched by the young woman. Slowly, both cautious of the other's intentions, they had grown to know each other and then had fallen in love. They knew it was dangerous, but the war would not last forever, and they talked about heading out of the state when his military obligations were over. One of his duties was leading reconnaissance missions to report the Seminoles' movements in the area. It was on one of these missions, shortly after the couple had shared their first kiss, that he was reported killed.

The Seminole woman heard what had happened and sat for days at the spring, crying for her fallen lover. It all became too much, and she weighed herself down and jumped in the water. The soldier, however, had survived the attack. Although it took him a few days to crawl back to the camp, he was alive and desperate to see the woman he intended to marry. But the other

This is what is left of the spring where the ghosts of the young soldier and the Seminole maiden are said to still try to find each other.

soldiers warned him not to go back to the spring. Someone had drowned in there, and the Seminoles in the area were convinced one of them had kidnapped an innocent woman and were desperate to get revenge. He at once knew who it was and rushed down, only to see her still floating in the water. He heard movement in the trees nearby, took out his sidearm and killed himself, falling into the water near her body.

The death happened in December or January, and people traveling to Fort King in those months are greeted by an unfamiliar fog that settles over only the spring. Mist is not unusual in Florida in those months, but those who have seen it describe it as localized and moving with intent, as if it has a personality. People who work there say fog is unusual anywhere in the park at any time of the year, except in that part of the woods. Today, it's not much more than an algae-covered water hole with no healing powers, but the spirits of the soldier and the woman are still seen on opposite sides of it, reaching out for each other but never allowed to touch. At times, they walk across the water toward each other, only to disappear before they can meet in the middle. Some visitors feel an odd sense of sadness while standing on the edge of the water, but only in those months. A semi-transparent figure dressed like a soldier is seen stumbling down the path from the main fort to the spring. It disappears when called.

It's a nice ghostly legend spread by historical reenactors who use the fort in those months, and the legend is retold by people following their visit to the fort. It echoes elements that folks are familiar with, a story that brings forth images of Romeo and Juliet and is repeated to explain the ghost lights at nearby Silver Springs. Two lovers are caught in the middle of violence. Because of a tragic series of events, their souls, still very much in love with each other, are stuck in an endless yearning that will never be satisfied. We would hate for that to happen to us, but its familiarity and message of love resonate with us. We believe that story. That would be just enough to make a ghost remain in the place where it died.

The other ghost story is not so simple and not nearly as endearing. Fort King is cursed, and the negative energy that has exploded at the base stretches its fingers down the streets and is said to be responsible for ghostly figures and weird things that happen there. Those stories, which are not the kind of tale you tell to tourists, come from the bloody history of the fort and are just as rational and understandable as those of the lost lovers.

"I've never heard that story," says Candice, who works at the fort. "But there are a lot of things going on here. You don't catch me here after dark." Unlike the spring, the fort is still strong, although that's an illusion. It has been destroyed and rebuilt several times; the current one now stands to honor the importance of the stronghold's place in Florida history more than to actually protect anything. Its colorful past began in 1827, when it was established as a garrison to protect Seminole lands from new people coming into the area, peacefully enforcing policies set by the Seminole Indian Agency across the street. Funding and shifting attitudes caused it to essentially close, but it was reopened a short time later, as President Andrew Jackson ordered the Seminoles to start moving from the state and into Oklahoma. Wiley Thompson was brought in to replace the kinder, gentler "Indian agent," and the fort was seen as the powder keg between the two sides.

Many Seminoles claimed that those who had signed treaties like the famous Treaty of Payne's Landing did not speak for the entire nation, and they refused to move. Tensions mounted, accompanied by smaller skirmishes that required both sides to reinforce their positions while continuing to sit down with each other and negotiate. Each side had one hand on the pen and the other on the sword. In late December 1835, American troops left Fort Brooks near Tampa to reinforce those at Fort King. They would never arrive. At what is now Bushnell, Florida, soldiers led by Major Francis Dade were ambushed; all but two were killed in what has been named the Dade Massacre.

What many people don't realize is that on the same day, Osceola, perhaps the most famous and vocal Seminole to oppose the move, attacked Wiley at Fort King, shooting him fourteen times, scalping him and taking out four other men in the process. As the Second Seminole War played itself out, the tribe burned the buildings of the fort to the ground, only to see it rebuilt a year later. It was finally abandoned in 1843, with people taking what was left of the fort to build houses, businesses and the Ocala courthouse.

While there is only a plaque and a small memorial to those who once were laid to rest there, those killed by Osceola and his men were buried in what is now the front park of the fort. As the war continued, other Americans killed nearby were also brought back to the fort for interment. That area is probably the most active at Fort King. Drivers traveling by at night see unexplained lights on the lawn. They hit websites to discuss walking their dogs at night and seeing soldiers there who disappear when they are approached. One man driving by during the day stopped on the side of the road because he thought the two men dressed in uniforms and carrying guns were part of a reenactment. To his surprise, the men slowly walked toward the woods and faded before his eyes. There are reenactments at Fort King, but they are scheduled events the city takes great pride in. They are not held in the middle of the week at five o'clock in the afternoon.

Candice has an explanation, which the people she works with share. "They took all of the bodies out and reburied them in the pyramid in St. Augustine. They say they got all the bodies, but there were houses built here already by the time they said they were able to reinter them." The pyramids she is referring to are the Dade Pyramids in the St. Augustine Post Cemetery,

The front lawn of Fort King, where bodies were dug up and people still see ghosts today.

which was designated a national cemetery in 1881. The memorial was originally paid for by the soldiers themselves when the government refused to fund it and holds the remains of soldiers who had died and were buried at other locations and then dug up and shipped to St. Augustine. It is one of the most famous haunted sites in a city known for its haunted locations. Both the violent and sudden deaths and the removal of the bodies are traditional sparks of ghostly activity. The spiritual reason for this may have to do with a soul returning and not finding peace because it cannot find its body.

The soldiers might not be the only spirits unable to find peace because their graves have been disturbed. While there are no written records, people, including archaeologists, believe there were people who inhabited that land before the Seminole and may have used that area for burial centuries before the ground was dug up and the first boards of Fort King were raised. In other words, bodies may have been removed to be replaced by other bodies, which were then removed. That means layers of restless souls. It's that added level, the one older than historical records, which makes some feel the whole area is now under some curse. "Some of the neighbors say some weird things happen here," says Candice. She explains that while people see odd lights and mysterious figures in different parts of the neighborhood, there are unexplained things that point to something other than ghosts. "There's a pretty high suicide rate within a couple-block radius here." Other people in the area point to continual closing and reopening and demolition and rebuilding in Ocala as further evidence of the curse. Even if that does not make sense to people on the outside, it is the kind of idea floated at Fort King and an example of the Ocala Syndrome. If bad things happen, blame it on the negative energy.

People like Ethan, who is not from the area, can only talk about the ghosts, which he feels are harmless. "I was walking around the structure telling my son about the history of the fort. I saw three men at the far entrance, near the gate that opens to the front of the park, carrying guns and walking slowly. One turned to look at me. They were far away, so I couldn't tell what they looked like, but I did see one had a thick moustache. They were not transparent or glowing. There was nothing strange about them." He thought there must be an event starting and rushed to see what they would be demonstrating. "I grabbed my son's hand, and we ran to catch them and see what they were doing. They were gone by the time we got there, but there was no place they could have snuck off to." While he admits it is possible they could have gone down a path or hidden from the father and son, he asked one of the rangers later if there was a special show happening.

Above: One of the places around the fort where mysterious people in uniform appear and disappear.

Opposite: The visitor's center at Fort King.

"The ranger said there was nothing planned. Then he stopped and looked at me. He gave me an odd smile and said, 'Don't worry. People see that kind of thing all the time here.'"

That's something Candice agrees with. Most of the employees have seen something or at least have heard a story from one of the visitors who has asked them to try and explain the moment. To her, the most haunted part of the memorial is the visitor's center. "There are many times I'm alone and something happens in different parts of the park. There have been some weird things that have happened on site near the visitor's center. There's knocking and then you're looking outside and no one's there. I try to ignore it, because the more I investigate it the louder it seems to get." She also reports that things have a habit of being moved or disappearing from the building, even when no one is there. Once, the knocking became so loud that she found it impossible to ignore and went to investigate. There was a violent smashing sound that she thought meant a tree had fallen on the visitor's center. She went outside to check it out, but there was no fallen tree and no natural reasons she should have heard the noise.

Logan works at many of the parks in the area. He has never seen anything himself but admits that there are too many stories to totally dismiss the possibility that Fort King is haunted. "It's one of those things that people talk about, and we had some investigators out once. We have a lot of reenactors come out and take a lot of pictures, and they get orbs and other things in them." His job is to lock up the parks, and he says he inherited that part of the job almost out of necessity. "Some of the guys won't walk the trails at night."

And then there is the haunted spring, the site of lost love, a mysterious fog and a ghost story that won't go away.

This is the kind of scene and story people talk about often, the kind that can't be backed up. In most cases it is because the legend is made up, but the activity is not. Logan has heard people tell the story but has never seen any lights coming from the area or heard any gunshots, despite being the person responsible for closing Fort King at night. "It's not like I don't believe it; there are things wrong with the story. I have never seen a fog at this fort. There is condensation sometimes, but I've never seen it get foggy [at the fort] or foggy down by the spring. It happens when the reenactors visit the site and they like to tell stories. It's what they do." And a good spooky tale should always have the element of, "It was a night just like tonight." Fort King is great for that. Whether it's the remains of a dug-up cemetery, the re-creation of destroyed armament or an overgrown watering hole, Fort King Park is the perfect spot to be the main character in any ghost story.

5

THE SAD STORY OF
MORRIS THE MAGICIAN

The feeling that Candice talks about, the weirdness and the unexplained, is shared by others in the city of Ocala. They tell the same kinds of stories about something being off and ghost stories being part of the personality of the town. Many, like Dave Schlenker's mom, feel Fort King is the source and that it spreads through the nearby neighborhoods and makes for some spooky sightseeing and storytelling. Schlenker, who wrote for the *Ocala Star-Banner* and used the paper to tell a few of Ocala's ghost stories over the years, talks of people experiencing phantoms and having unusual things happen. They chalk it up to being part of the Ocala. "We lived a little over a mile from Fort King. We started to have weird things happen in our house. Little things that were on the shelf would magically appear on the floor or different places." He wrote about another ghost who mysteriously emptied the garbage one night. His mother named the ghost Ralph, after her brother-in-law. Its origin had two possible explanations. "She used to say, 'I bet you I picked up a ghost going by the old fort.'"

At other times, she had another explanation. "I attribute it to some mischievous brothers. My mom got an imagination working at the theater and blamed it on Morris." His family members are not the only people who speak of the old Ocala Civic Theatre and the magician who came to town in the late 1940s with the intention of building a place dedicated to his life's work. "Everyone, all the old-timers, all had a story. Pranks. Doors being shut or moving vases," says Schlenker. "A lot of time when people were alone there they just got the feeling they weren't. I think a lot of it had to do with the legends in the back of their mind. But some of it didn't."

This ghost story is more of a love story. That might sound strange, but take a moment and think about some of the most well-known haunted legends or true ghost stories you've heard. Many of their elements are the same as a love story, and many of them find their roots deep in love somehow. Love compels us when we are alive, so why should that same intense emotion not be the reason a spirit stays in a location? We understand a good ghost story the same way we understand a love story, so it only makes sense that the two should often go hand in hand.

It involves a woman named Katherine and her husband, Morris, a legend in Ocala who dreamed of being the world's greatest magician. They loved each other, but Morris was also enamored with a building that is no longer standing. The lot on East Silver Springs Boulevard is nothing now but additional parking for the local Sonny's restaurant. But seventy years ago, it looked very different. This tale takes place before the torn-down building was the Marion County Republican headquarters and even before the street was lined with chain restaurants and stores. Instead, imagine a theater. Rick Allen, another writer for the *Ocala Star-Banner* and the unofficial authority on Morris Osborn, says the town was different when the Morris Osborn After-Dinner Theater opened. "At the time it was built, there was nothing there. It's now a Mecca of commerce, but back then it really stood out."

Most of what we know of the magician and his lovely wife and assistant comes from a one-hundred-page book she wrote about him so that the children and grandchildren would remember him. Allen was able to get many of the details for his readers when the original building was being torn down in 2016. Morris was born in nearby Alachua County in 1899 but moved to New York as an adult to try to make his fortune. While working for an advertising agency, he met the love of his life, Katherine, often referred to as Kay by those who knew her well. Although she was twenty years younger than him, Kay was intrigued by Morris and encouraged him to move back to Florida to pursue his dreams of being a world-famous illusionist. During his life, he gained a modest following and is said to have invented several tricks and devices still used today, including the Acrobatic Thimbles and the Third Hand.

The couple moved back to Florida and tried their hand at several ventures, often relying on Kay's income to help finance his dreams of stardom. She believed in him and was willing to sacrifice. According to Allen, they ran a dance club, a dry-cleaning chain and a snake and chicken farm while touring

The parking lot where Morris Osborn once performed magic.

the state as a magic act known as Morris and the Maids. Morris sometimes went by the name Sohmer the Mystical. "He was the showy one, and she was the backbone. She put in the hard work, and he got to do all the flashy stuff." They also made friends with Ross Allen (no relation), the infamous animal handler and showman who was helping to put Silver Springs on the map. "He always admired those magicians who had their own theater," says Rick Allen, who tells of Morris speaking with the famous Dante the Magician to get ideas and inspiration for opening his After-Dinner Theater. "Then when he got here, he was finally able to do it." It was not a grand venture made with the finest materials and with attention paid to every detail. Instead, it was pieced together with what they could afford, including used seats, but with a master plan. It was designed with Morris's act specifically in mind, so the angles were based on his illusions. The details, like a trapdoor and the right lighting to make the act work, were built into the plans. Morris was in his element and oversaw everything, and with each board put up and nail hammered in, he came closer to seeing his dream fulfilled.

According to Rick Allen, for only $1.25, people were allowed to enter the Morris Osborn After-Dinner Theater and see his inaugural show, *The Girl from Nowhere*. It was a family affair, as his wife and children were also part of the show. All reports indicate that the first performance went well. Morris's banter and work with the crowd won him over, and the people of Ocala overlooked the shabby setting for a fun night of magic. The second show, it is said, was not as well received. Morris and Katherine were not sure why, but despite the magician giving it his all, he could not connect, and he did not feel the same energy from the audience he had fed off of in that first show. Legend says he was so shaken by the bad performance that he was hospitalized just a few days later. He recovered and a reopening was planned, but a short time before, Katherine hosted a party for the crew and helpers. The party was also attended by her friend Ethal Boyce, a former fortune-teller and psychic. She had a bad feeling for Morris and the theater. Within a few days, Morris suffered a heart attack and died at Munroe Hospital.

Morris, the romantic historians of the town claim, had died of a broken heart. After working his adult life trying to build his dream, he passed at fifty-four just as it was becoming a reality. Others remember the story differently with the benefit of time, despite factual evidence to the contrary. They say Morris actually died on stage, making it even more convincing that he should come back and haunt the building he erected. Either way, the venue became home to the Marion Players shortly after his death and burial at nearby Island Memorial Park. Almost immediately, Morris's ghost began to take center stage.

The Marion Players did little to improve the building when they took over, and it may have been the rundown, thrown-together nature of the structure that both endeared it to the locals and supplied tales of the ghost. They kept the trapdoor, something the actors would often stumble over. The restrooms were too close to the stage, so anyone going to the bathroom during a performance became part of the show. Dave Schlenker says there was often movement near the stage that had nothing to do with the prankster spirit. "They used to say the curtains would move during the show, and everyone there knew it was because of the rats." It was the kind of place just bad enough to be endeared by the people who went there, even as the years passed and it was renamed the Ocala Civic Theatre. As it was being readied to be torn down in 2016, people began sharing their memories. The more they did, the more people remembered Morris's ghost along with their show experiences. "When they tore down the old theater, that's when a lot of the old stories started to resurface. Then they'd talk about Morris. People who were old-timers over there just all knew. If anything weird happened, they'd say, 'Yeah, that's just Morris.'"

It is a cliché that all theaters are haunted. Actors and directors are a superstitious lot, making sure they never mention the title of the play *Macbeth*, that people don't whistle and that one light is always left on for any ghosts who might haunt a theater. No one needed to leave a light on for Morris Osborn after he died. He had a habit of turning the lights on himself, even if it was during a show. Rick Allen was told one odd story from an old crew member. "He and another person were in the light booth, and they weren't quite paying attention the way they should have been. They missed the light cue, but the lights went up on their own." At other times, people would shut everything off, only to have them mysteriously turned back on when they went back to lock the doors for the night.

Dave Schlenker grew up hearing the stories, because his mother worked at the theater. He wanted to be an actor from an early age, so her way to help was to get a job there. "My mom got to know the theater crowd really well just to make sure I would be safe over there. She ended up becoming the box office manager. She spent a lot of time in the old theater, often alone in the box office. She didn't have any use for ghost stories, and she'd hear these stories and just roll her eyes." Then one night while working late and with the place empty, she heard clanging. She went to where the sound had come from, but there was no one there. She could hear talking and whispering from different places in the darkness but could not see anyone. "It changed her mind on the whole ghost thing. She was convinced there was something weird going on." From that day on, she experienced little things to reinforce the idea that Morris was still around. "She would come home and say, 'You'll never guess what Morris did today.' Just casually mention it." His mother also told of other women she worked with who had spent time there alone, gotten spooked and left. They would not tell what happened to them.

In the spirit of a true performer, Morris never interfered with what was happening on the stage in a negative way, but that did not stop him from showing up when the curtain closed. "He was very wisely marketed," says Schlenker. "If you go there you might see the ghost. Nobody was scared; it

The new theater in Ocala, where Morris is no longer seen.

was widely known there was a harmless ghost." Some who came forward to share their stories while the venue was being torn down talked of odd knocks on the bathroom wall during intermissions. Several people talked of seeing someone walking around the rafters before and after shows, who would then disappear. Actors would sometimes say they saw him in the dressing room or on the stage. "It was always part of the landscape of that theater," says Schlenker, who believes that Morris might be real but was probably exaggerated by people in the theater who then nursed the legend. "These are theater people. They like drama and to expound the mysteries."

By the 1970s, the theater's name was changed to the Ocala Civic Theatre, and when a new facility opened down the street in 1988, people wondered what would happen to Morris. Some assumed he would follow the arts, and there were a few reports of odd things happening in the new building. That may have been more memory than magician and a product of people trying to link history. Today, no one there talks of ghosts. Others felt that Morris might stick around when his building became the new headquarters for the Marion County Republican Party. Both Ross and Schlenker feel there were things that happened there the tenants would not talk about, but no one would officially talk to them about it.

As generations pass, Morris Osborn might one day fade from memory. William Shakespeare was known for his plays, the kind that once graced the stage in Ocala. But there's a line from one of his sonnets that the old entertainer might have enjoyed more. "So long as men can breathe, or eyes can see, / So long lives this, and this gives life to thee." As long as someone is still around to talk of the accountant turned husband and father turned reptile handler turned magician turned ghostly legend, he will always be part of the town.

6

THE STIKINI

Lee Ehrlich, the paranormal investigator from GhostPro, has had several experiences in the Ocala National Forest, most of which he attributes to ghosts and spirits of one kind or another. When asked about his most unusual experiences, he transitions to talking about beasts in the woods or, more specifically, unexplained supernatural creatures that call the forest home. His simplest answer, if his answer can be called simple, is that they involve a Skunk Ape, Florida's version of Bigfoot. The real story might be something even more unusual and connected with the paranormal history of the state.

One night, he and about a dozen other men set up near a sinkhole on Pat's Island near the famous Yearling Trail. They set up a fire, but then something odd, about the size of a raccoon, crawled out of the woods. "It looked like a mist, like smoke. It ran into our campsite and jumped into the fire. Then it danced around in circles and took off back into the woods." He attributes what he saw to some kind of spirit animal, perhaps of something that had been killed when the sinkhole was used by Native Americans in the area as a hunting ground. "They would run through the forest after deer and force them in that direction. They would run down the slope, which was so big you could fit three or four houses down there. They would shoot them like fish in a barrel." Another night, he saw what may have been another spirit animal in the same area. "I got up one night to go to the bathroom. It was pitch-black, and I didn't have a flashlight. I could hear these feet, like walking uphill towards me, scuffing towards me. From the sinkhole there was

A place in the Ocala near where Lee Ehrlich saw his ghost animals.

this rustling. Then what looked like a full-grown deer leapt out of nowhere. It took one or two strides and then disappeared."

Another night, he and some investigators were camping nearby. They were exploring some of the abandoned cemeteries and old Cracker homes and had just laid their tents and bags for the night. Something out there had different plans for them. They began to hear knocking sounds on trees, which many Skunk Ape authorities closely relate to the creature. They responded by knocking back, but then it became more sinister. According to Ehrlich, whatever was out there was forcing them into the tents rather than trying to engage the men. "Some creature corralled us into our tents. It surrounded us in such a way that there had to be more than one of them. It was just moving too fast. Something then dragged its claws down the side of it. You could see its hands making imprints in the fabric."

While the experienced investigator is slow to offer a definitive answer to what he saw, his story is echoed by many who spend time in the Ocala. There are common factors when people share their stories or talk about what other people have told them. Almost always, the person is experienced in the woods and knows animals. They report that there is something not normal about what they have seen; it is not an ordinary animal. Much like the Ocala Shift, there is something otherworldly about them. People associate what they have seen with the real animals or supernatural beasts they know. What Ehrlich experienced that night, the corralling and the scrapes on his tent, may have been another monster altogether, which the Seminoles call the Stikini.

It starts with a goddess who came to be known as "She Who Walks the Circle." She started her life as a normal person. Betrayed by love, she called on the gods to give her the power to get back at the man who had thrown away her love. They granted her request, but she did not stop at the man who scorned her. Once he got what was coming to him, she moved on to other men who had hurt women, then to men whom she suspected might cause pain in the future. With each murder, she became less human, until she was nothing more than a monster, forced to walk around in a circle, cutting into the land and creating an unknown lake with her tears.

The location, however, was well known to other Seminole maidens who had also been hurt by love. One by one, they made their way to her, praying to her to give them her power to get revenge. She granted them their wish, and off they went with the same vengeance in their eyes that she once had. Some stopped with the object of their hate, but a few fell into the same temptation she had given in to. Legend has it that She Who Walks the Circle was all too happy to entice them into giving into their need for revenge. They took their plots too far and became hungry with the power she had given them. Like her, they fell into the curse, and every death stripped away a little more of their humanity until they were no longer recognizable as women. They had become the Stikini.

These monsters, still said to be active in and around the Ocala, are blood-drinking, flesh-eating vampires. Often beautiful and alluring by day,

On the road from the Ocala to Tampa, where the Stikini are said to stalk.

they turn into mysterious, human-and-owl-like creatures at night. They must feed on the entrails and blood of men and sometimes store the men they capture to eat later or to make into stew. (Almost no versions involve women being victimized.) They can change into their wicked selves at will but cannot stand the light of day as the creature. They patrol the dark woods, areas off the beaten path and swamps, looking for prey. They have little or no knowledge of their past lives or what caused them to change into the abomination in the first place. They seek out one another and live in a coven, which hints more at the story's European influence than a traditional Native American narrative. Isolated from the main tribe, they travel the woods looking for victims.

The creatures are the things that nightmares are made of and are an excellent folklore warning against greed and sexual assault. However, the story told about them is odd in terms of storytelling. The women are the ones who were wronged, even if they eventually gave into their impulses and went too far. In more modern versions, people are warned to avoid the woods, not to avoid hurting women. The Stikini are more sinned against than sinning, which makes one wonder whom exactly these stories are meant to warn.

Maybe it's just a story—except for the fact that people are still seeing them in the woods today. Maggie has spent time walking near the ghost town of Kismet near Altoona and Alexander Spring. More than once, she has seen something unexplained that she attributes to an evil witch. "There's not much out there, but my boyfriend and I did find a cemetery. It's kind of a dark place; you feel it. The first time, we were just looking around. Twice I saw what I thought was a dark figure out of the corner of my eye. I'd look and nothing. Both times, this is messed up. Both times there was an owl there." Maggie claims that, another time, she was told where to find the headstones by a website that specializes in ghost towns across Florida. But she was surprised to see two people, dressed in thick black robes despite the heat, where GPS indicated the graves would be. "I was scared, but he said we were too far away to be seen. I convinced him to drive away. We drove away, but I was still looking at them through the window with only a few trees in the way." With a broken voice, she explained that, as she watched, both figures flew into the sky with a screech.

The Stikini are more famously seen on the west side of the forest, more specifically in the woods that extend out of the Ocala to Tampa. The story that connects it to Fort King begins almost two hundred years ago.

On December 23, 1835, 110 men set out from Fort Brook north to Fort King. Fort King had been subject to attacks in the preceding months as the U.S. government struggled to move the Seminole tribe west to Oklahoma, something some Seminole leaders had agreed to without the consent of all of those in control of the multiple factions that made up the complex nation. The military march was led by Major Francis Langhorne Dade, who decided to take charge when the original commander was confronted with problems on the home front. They made their way down King's Highway, a narrow path through wilderness and swamp designed specifically to connect the two locations. Destroyed bridges and artillery too heavy for the journey plagued them and slowed the trip, something the Seminoles had facilitated in an attempt to slow the expedition. Osceola, recognized as one of their major leaders, was in negotiations that he expected to lose, but he had set a trap as the Seminoles waited to hear word from him.

On December 28, as the U.S. troops marched with their guns under heavy coats near what is now Bushnell, Florida, they were attacked by almost twice as many Seminoles hidden in the swamps and perched behind trees. When the battle was over, all but three of the soldiers and their guide had been killed. The Seminoles had made a statement about not being so easily moved from their land, and the seeds of the Second Seminole War had been planted. History tells of Ransom Clarke, who survived and crawled sixty-five miles to get back to Fort Brooke. Private Edward Decourcey is remembered for hiding under dead bodies and then being killed when he and Clarke were attacked on their way back and split up in order to force their pursuer to choose between them. And then there was an illiterate private who somehow managed to make it out alive. No one can really get a handle on his part in the battle or how he made it back to Fort Brooke, but Joseph Sprague also lived through the attack.

Private Joseph Sprague is an odd footnote in history. He is cited in a few sources as being a survivor of the Dade Massacre but is missing from most of the definitive books and articles. Sprague was a career military man from Vermont who kept enlisting because he was not qualified to do much more than be a grunt. After each campaign, he was granted a little bit of land and a pension but could not make things work. He signed up again, leaving only an X as a signature, and fought another battle without distinction or merit. During the Dade Massacre, he hid under dead bodies after the initial attack and was left for dead when a troop of Black Seminoles came along after the battle to kill off anyone still alive and raid for anything useful. Sprague crawled the rest of the way to Fort Brooke and reported what had happened the day after Ransom Clarke made it home. Clarke, the more articulate and literate of the two, has gone down in history as the only survivor of the day. History has all but forgotten Sprague.

According to Stikini lore, however, Sprague was a deserter who was the only man able to fully explain what they said really happened that winter. The website Folktales of Florida summarizes the story:

> Through the first Seminole War a small group of elderly Seminole women were allowed to remain in their homes on North of Fort Brooke on the Hillsborough River. In 1835 The United States moved forward with plans to relocate all of the Seminole Indians west of the Mississippi. When given this news, these woman were enraged, refused to move and threatened that Fort Brooke would be forever cursed. Soon thereafter, 110 soldiers left Ft Brooke moving Northward. The first morning at camp a young soldier was found dead in his bed, an investigation concluded that the man's heart had been removed. This same scenario happened night after night and as fear of the Seminole women's curse grew stronger, soldier Joseph Sprague abandoned his post. As he fled through the forest at dusk he saw the group of Seminole Women whom had cursed the soldiers. He watched in horror as they kneeled, chanted and expelled their internal organs from their mouths. One by one they then took the form of owls and took off into the night. They were the stikini witches of Seminole legend coming to exact their revenge. Sprague hurried the news to Fort Brooke but by the time reinforcements arrived all 109 other soldiers lay dead in their beds with their hearts removed. The group of elderly Seminole were never seen again but will always be remembered in this story of the Dade Massacre.

It's an odd story, especially considering that the massacre is both well documented and a victory for the Seminoles. There is little reason to make up a supernatural story for it. The best explanation is that something like the Stikini has been seen along the path between the two forts and the folklore is working its way backward.

The more recent legends are a mix of ghost stories and unexplained beast sightings, the perfect trail for the witches to walk on. Samantha has been searching for an explanation behind one odd night she shared with her friends on the Silver River, which roughly runs near the route of the Dade Massacre Stikini. "My friends and I were boating and got stranded on the Silver River one night. We hadn't been talking, it was late, and we had a couple of lines in the water making the most of being stranded. About 2:00 a.m. we heard a 'scream,' bloodcurdling. [It] sounded like a high-pitched woman's scream ending in this low, guttural growl that reverberated and rattled our teeth. We heard nothing approach and nothing leave, no wings, no leaves rustling, no branches…nothing. So, when the scream occurred, we all just about just died right on the spot. Frozen, we were stuck to the spot and couldn't go anywhere even if we wanted to."

Della Daughtry's representation of the Stikini. *Courtesy of Della Daughtry.*

Samantha went on to describe that they all felt that whatever was there was angry about them being in the area. Places near the Ocala are famous for unexplained noises in the night that might have an explanation during the day, and the Silver River has a history of escaped monkeys, but the people on the boat that night were not scared novices. All had spent time in the woods and on the water at night, and one friend had spent time in the Everglades as an airboat tour guide and had worked at Silver Springs running a jeep tour. What makes Samantha's story point at the Seminole witches is the words she chose when asked what might have been there with them. "A forest banshee, a restless witch spirit?"

Logan also has been looking for something to explain what happened to him and his friends almost a decade ago in the woods, and his tale echoes Samantha's. When he was a teen, he and his friends were driving around in trucks in the woods of Ocklawaha. "We went down this one trail. We've never really recalled being there as it was overgrown. All four trucks died a few seconds apart. All trucks shut off, wouldn't start at all and our phones were just static when we tried to make a call." While most of the trucks were older and used as off-road vehicles, one was fairly new and had less than ten thousand miles on it. They began to hear invisible dogs barking all around them, especially odd given there were no houses nearby. They all got into the newer truck and locked the doors. "Eventually after about two hours, it stopped. The phones were working, trucks started right up. Come daylight, we went outside and found scratch marks down the side of the Silverado."

The scratches were in sets of three, much like an owl who had four talons but with one toward the back.

The entire time they were trapped, they heard no noises on the truck or saw anything outside the window. It's his previous experience in the forests that leads Logan to believe it was not just a random animal. "I've seen people just standing in the middle of the forest dead of night, just staring at you, then in the blink of an eye they're gone."

"These small towns, we grew up in, our parents grew up in. We've all heard stories from our parents, from our grandparents. When you're ten you think it's complete crap just to scare the kids. Until you experience it yourself. People like us have always hunted there and fished there and partied out there. You're dead center in the forest. You see things, you hear it. Some experiences you share, some you brush off and some you never speak of again."

7

THE CURSE OF
THE COYOTE WOMAN

Some ghostly legends just don't make sense, but the fact that they are told and believed make them impossible to ignore. When you hear them, the commonsense trigger in your brain goes off. There are too many holes. The details don't add up. The characters do the same thing somewhere else, and the setting is just too perfect.

But then there is the sincerity of the teller, passing the story down to you the way it was passed down to him or her, and you can hear the belief in their voice. Maybe the story can't be believed, but the storyteller can. Then you get to the end, and the person tells you their own experience. After taking a moment to think about how easy it is to have something happen when you already think a place is haunted, you're left with that sensation in your gut that something about all of it must be true. When you're dealing with a haunted cemetery hidden in the trees of a forgotten town in the Ocala, you just nod and understand that it's true enough.

If you look at a map of Florida and search for the town of Rosewood, you're going to be disappointed. Search for it on the internet and see what you can find, but you'll spend time looking into the wrong place in a nearby community. Focus on a small town named Paisley and run your finger down Old Cemetery Road; somewhere before you reach Lake Dorr is a small cemetery, overgrown and unattended, where a young woman committed suicide because of love. Her death can't be confirmed. The existence of the town of Rosewood in Lake County can't be confirmed. The cemetery is there, however, so the story is still being passed down.

Della Daughtry's representation of the Coyote Woman. *Courtesy of Della Daughtry.*

Young love is both pure and foolish, which might be why the teens fell in love so easily and ignored the fact that they might be causing trouble by being together. It was not that she was only fifteen and he was almost a man at seventeen, but the fact that she was White and he was Black. And it was not as if she came from a progressive family. Her father was an angry man, and when he found out that the two young people were seeing each other, he threated to kill the young man. After cooling down, he tried sending her away or disowning her, but the girl's mother couldn't stand not having her close, and she fought to keep her at home. The father gave in but silently fumed, still demanding they stop seeing each other. So, the couple grew careful. They met in secret in an old cemetery in a part of the woods where they could be away from the glaring eyes of the community and the anger of her father.

The fire was still burning in her father's belly. One day, he saw the young man in the center of Rosewood, and he viciously beat him in front of onlookers, who did nothing to stop it. He then dragged the boy into the woods to finish the job. The young lover was never seen again. In later years, people said the young man took off for South Florida or left the state altogether. Others say he died in the woods, either hanged or buried where no one would find him. What is known is that the girl found out about the beating and made her way to town to try to find her father and her lover. She was overwhelmed by the amount of blood at the site where the fight had taken place. Those who hadn't intervened were now avoiding eye contact with her. She vowed then to get her revenge.

Her father always kept a revolver in his nightstand, and when he returned home, he found his daughter standing in the kitchen, waiting for him with his gun pointed at him. She shot him. As the emotional girl began to think of a world without the man she loved and having to face her mother after killing her father, she broke down and ran to the cemetery. She waited, half expecting her boyfriend to come crashing through the trees. As time went by, she cried and cried until her voice took on the sound of a coyote. She then laid on one of the graves and took her own life with the gun.

On the road to the Coyote Woman's cemetery.

But that's not where the story ends. Her body was never found. People say she instantly transformed into a coyote and continues to walk the woods. She is known to attack and kill evil-spirited people she finds in the forest, taking revenge on those who stood by and did nothing to save the helpless man years ago. There are some who say she laid down a curse—that's why the town burned down a short time later and has been erased from the history books. The howls of the coyotes in that part of Ocala are different. Those from the area, no strangers to unexplained sounds in the trees, say that, at times, you can still hear her cries in their nightly calls.

Taylor tells the story with a mix of conviction and doubt often seen when people retell something odd that happened to them and that they need someone—anyone—to know about. He has spent his whole life running into the unexplained in the Ocala, but this one sticks with him. "It's just old folklore. I have no way to prove it, and it's only hearsay around these parts. This is what I was told as a boy." The story came down to him from the previous generation, who had the name of the town and the legend passed down to them. "It's something we talk about when it's brought up by the older generation, but most people my age or younger know little to nothing about it."

The cemetery in question might actually have a name. There is only one along the path Taylor talks about, and until recently, there was no way to find it unless you already knew it was there. If you're familiar with the trail he used to walk or drive his off-road vehicles on and the trails the hunters still take, you might be able to find it. It is considered a road, although no one new to the area can tell that from the narrow path it takes through the thick trees, throwing passengers around as they make their way over random bumps and potholes while trying to avoid thick tree roots blocking the way. If your car or truck can make it there, you will come across Maple Grove Cemetery, also known as Shockley Cemetery.

It's as forgotten as the township nearby that used to bear the name of the people buried there. Shockley Cemetery got its name from the only remaining headstone among the small markers too worn to read. This is the spot where Hinkley and Anne Shockley are laid to rest. They came from Milan, Indiana, in the 1800s in a failed attempt to heal Anne's tuberculosis, and the community known as Shockley Hills developed around their homestead. The fence that now surrounds them is not an accurate border for all who might be buried there, as more were known to have been laid to rest there but are now lost to the forest. Two trees fell years ago, crushing the fence and all but hiding what remains of the graves. All you can see as you walk by is a large obelisk, looking foreign among the trees. The Shockleys, and for that matter Shockley Hills, now exist only if people are willing to dig.

The same can be said about the town Taylor says his family talked about. There is no record of a Rosewood in that area, something not uncommon in that area of Florida. As they boomed and failed, unincorporated sections would take the name of materials that came from the area or the name of the founder. The name persists throughout Lake County and neighboring regions. You'll find streets and businesses named Rosewood; apartment communities and retirement homes also bear the name. It might be a

What is left of Shockley Cemetery.

misremembering of names like Rosebush and Ridgewood, both of which can be found on old phosphorus and train maps.

Then there is the story of the actual Rosewood, Florida, a town that represents all that is wrong with race relations in the state. In short, Francis Taylor, a White woman living in Sumter, accused a Black man of assaulting her in her house early in 1923. While much of her claim was later refuted, it was enough to inflame area residents. By the time the mob formed, the charge included rape. Sheriff Elias Walker, the main character in many of the legends and folklore of the area, began deputizing men. The crowd grew to over one hundred men. They brought search dogs into neighboring Rosewood, a predominantly African American community, to retrieve the prime suspect, Aaron Carrier. He was delivered back to the jail, but the still amped-up mob returned to the town to get Sam Carter, a man accused of other crimes. Sam Carter ended up being shot, his body hung as a message to the town. The mob returned a few days later and was met with gunfire as it tried to storm Aaron Carrier's aunt's house, which they believed held fugitives who had recently escaped from jail and those who had helped them. When everything was over, at least eight people were dead, although unofficial numbers put the death toll as high as one hundred. The town was burned down, just like the forgotten town in Lake County.

It's an often-ignored moment in Florida history, brought up again in 1997 when late writer and director John Singleton made a movie about it and shot parts of it in Lake County, not far from where the cemetery is. Some details have played themselves out in other communities nearby, like the clash between White citizens and African American miners in Dunnellon in 1895. That story ended with the overmatched miners fighting back, only to be killed and dumped in the Withlacoochee River. Minor incidents of racial tension that escalated to murders and the burnings of whole communities can be marked off on a map of Florida like stains on history.

It can't be ignored in the story of the Coyote Woman. While the town probably would have existed before the massacre, the racial elements of the story may have led to the adoption of the famous town's name over the years. At first glance, it feels like it should be a Native American story because of the coyote; instead, the couple is a White girl and a Black boy. If there is some truth to the story (or at least a reason for the early storytellers to make a statement on race), it makes sense for Rosewood to be adopted as the unnamed town.

There is another issue with the legend. The way Taylor tells the story, the woman died a long time ago, long enough for there to be no record of the story, the deaths or the town. Yet coyotes are not native to Florida. In fact, the animals have been in the area for only a few decades. The first consistent reports date to the mid- to late 1970s. If you ask hunters in that part of the woods, they will tell you that there is something else fitting the description. Florida panthers, especially females, sound like other big cats but also register in a pitch that sounds very similar to the scream of a woman. It is the reason why so many locations across the country, including the Ocala, have rumors of banshees, the mystical women of ghost stories who lure men into the woods with their cries in order to kill them.

None of this matters to Taylor and others who have experienced the strange woman. While there are no reports of people seeing her, they believe she hunts out there and may be responsible for some of the people who disappear in the Ocala. They have also heard her unusual cry. "I can only attest to us growing up there. You could be all alone and hear a crying howl or in a group and it would still happen. Could hear the sound of a girl crying within the screaming howl." He's not a tourist to the woods and has spent enough time there to be able to identify most of the animal noises he hears. Anyone who spends time in the forest near there will notice that it is not like other places. The familiar can quickly become unfamiliar.

"The air feels different; it moves and sounds different. The best way to experience [the forest] is to stay out there a night or two, on a full moon when animals and nature are most active. You can ride the trails and hunt for years and still get lost and think you're on a different trail, but never left the one you were on. Time even moves different there. It's hard to explain, but when you're in the middle of it, deep in the wetlands or riding through the cemetery, you really do feel something."

The young lover must know this, too. She now walks among the trees and animals, looking for the bad people and paying for her sins. Time is different for her; she is not allowed to move on or find peace. Instead, she cries, and the locals who can ignore the old burned foundations and the feeling of being watched are forced to know her sadness.

8

CEMETERIES, CELERY AND SERIAL KILLERS IN SANFORD

anford is known to be haunted. Ask residents or any of the half dozen companies that run ghost tours through the city that has been called the best place to live in Florida. The city has both urban and country aspects, and the haunted stories its residents tell have the same feel. It's the epicenter of the infamous Dead Zone of I-4, a legend told of cars and electronics going wacky on the main highway across the state. While building the road, engineers and crews cut through Timucua mounds or burial sites of old residents, depending on who is telling the story. Then there are the ghosts of New Tribes Mission, where the evil spirits of Starke Prison's executed killers, including Ted Bundy, are said to travel through the electrical wires and torment people.

In a city that so embraces its ghosts, there is one story that connects its history with the paranormal more than any other: the story of a horse, a cheapskate and a burial mound that should have been left alone.

Several stories are told about local blacksmith Sligh Ernest and his giant horse. Most of the tales feel like details made up to fill in the holes someone has pointed out. The most well-known version, the one told by Charlie Carlson in his book *Weird Florida* and then retold by others, like ghost story authority Mark Muncy, is that Ernest's prized horse died and needed to be hauled through town to be buried. It was enormous, over three thousand pounds, and stood over seven feet tall. It was white and beautiful. The horse died. But it did not stay dead for long.

The view from Celery Road.

It may have been upset at the way it was dragged and discarded at burial or the fact that it trampled a mound where Timucua had buried their dead. It came back to haunt the town when the road was widened and its own grave was upset.

That doesn't make sense. How wide was the road in the first place? Why did they not just bury the horse farther away or someplace nowhere near the road?

Questions are stones that cause legends to shift, and on Celery Road, the story has changed over the decades. Ernest was cheap. He was traveling into town when the horse collapsed unexpectedly. Ernest dug a grave where he stood to save money. This version leaves out the stirring image of the carriages coming to the homestead to lug the dead beast away, but it makes more sense. It also explains why a burial area might have been disturbed, much like the tale told about I-4.

Regardless of the origin story, the horse has been spotted since the road was expanded, and reports keep coming in. In *Weird Florida*, Carlson records several witnesses who experienced the horse running down the road and disappearing. Another of his stories touched on a Native American in a headdress riding on top of the old stallion and keeping up with the moving car before vanishing. Some of the most disturbing versions involve a man on top of the horse with a black void instead of features for a face. Witnesses sense anger coming from both the mount and the rider as it attacks them.

There is a more modern version of the story. All the same players are there, but in recent days, another, a sadder story has been making the rounds on the internet. It may be a clear case of a haunted location taking on the form of another, similar legend, but there have been a few posts that say the horse is being chased by the man, who struggles to keep up. Each time he gets close, the horse disappears; he yells and then fades himself. The story, called the "Tale of the Traveler," is told by Creek and tribes from Nevada. He was a man who loved his horse but was known as a shrewd businessman who would often trick people into paying too much for his services. Through cunning, bravery and sketchy dealings, he amassed a herd of horses everyone else in the tribe envied. Then someone he had crossed cursed him. One day, the Traveler went out to his field and found an old, gray, ugly horse he could not remember. Annoyed, he beat the horse until it was dead. That night, it came back as a beautiful, giant white horse. It had changed itself to see if the man was truly worthy to own them, and he failed miserably. The spirit horse had stolen all of them and taken them to a faraway place and would only give them back if the man could catch it. With that, the ghost steed sped off, and the man followed. For three days and nights the man trailed but could never catch the phantom. Several times he saw his herd, but it always disappeared when he got too close. On the third day, the Traveler collapsed. The ghost horse carried him back to his land, which was now worthless. A few weeks later, the man died with no beasts, no money and no friends. His soul remains trapped, still trying to catch the horse and learn his lesson and earn his honor back.

The tales of haunted cemeteries in Sanford are also not your straightforward ghost stories. A cemetery haunting usually has a backstory, such as a mysterious person seen at night or a secret mourner who disappears after people see him or her walking from headstone to headstone. They are based on our fears about the afterlife, the place where people should be at

The entrance to Shiloh Cemetery.

rest and find peace. If they wander, then we may wander when we die. So witnesses make up a story with the rows of characters in front of them, and if there is something about a grave that draws their attention, that's the best suspect. The mysterious woman in black belongs to the cracked grave nearby with four smaller stones placed beside her. She must have lost her children and returns at night to find them. It all makes perfect sense, and the unexplained is in some small way explained.

This might be why the ghost seen at Shiloh Cemetery seems so unusual. People can't find an easy story. Out of the vacuum instead comes a tale that doesn't line up but has become known throughout the community anyway. The descriptions of the Lady of Shiloh are so unusual and yet so specific that it makes sense people need to create stories to explain her. Instead of a woman in a white, flowing gown, she is dressed in dark robes that hide her body and shade her actual height. Some of the stories say that you can't see her feet, so she appears to be floating. What really defines her, however, is her long hair, flowing as if by an invisible wind. That, and the fact that her face is nothing more than a skull, sometimes with flaps of skin still attached. "I've seen every horror movie ever," says Amber, who has spotted the woman during the day and once when she and her friends went out investigating ghosts. "Her face doesn't look like she's decomposed. The skin looks eaten away. Maybe the story makes me think that, I guess. You've heard the story?"

The Lady of Shiloh walks around the tree lines but has also been seen near different headstones. She is described as not interested in where she is, as if she would haunt this place no matter what it was. Maybe that is because Shiloh looks as though someone was trying to learn how to make a burial ground and used the land for practice. The headstones are falling apart and crooked. The land has evidence that people have been through on dirt bikes and off-road vehicles, with tracks weaving in and out of markers and then back into the woods. Fragments of stones and memorials and weatherworn crosses are thrown into piles. Slabs are rising out of the ground as if trying to dig their way out; others are tossed into the woods or are so overgrown they can barely be found.

She does not normally interact with people but floats around, night and day, detached and appearing like a movie projected against the wrong background. Then she is gone, and those who witness her say they did not mistake her for a trick of light or a product of their imagination. They saw something; the only issue is who she might be.

Shiloh Cemetery itself does not offer much in terms of an explanation. It is one of five plots of land collectively known as Sanford Cemetery, the largest and most modern of which is Evergreen Municipal Cemetery, which faces West Twenty-Fifth Street with a clean, majestic front. The resting place presents a well-organized if generic spot, something you pass by without thinking too much about it. In fact, if you didn't know there was something older beyond it, you would never guess that behind the newer cemeteries are two that are falling apart and neglected. They are highly vandalized and were lost to history for decades until recent interest from the community sparked their rejuvenation. As you leave the well-paved roads that outline Evergreen and move farther back, there is a greater difference in the styles of the burial grounds and the way they are maintained. Go deeper, and more ghost stories come out. The graves start to become more fractured and overrun with growth. Trash piles up, as if the worst of the front cemeteries has blown back to the older ones, hoping that history can be brushed away as easily.

Maybe the Lady of Shiloh walks over from the Page-Jackson Cemetery. That's been known to happen. The burial ground is now hailed as a crucial

One of the more popular places to see the Lady of Shiloh.

link to the history of African Americans in the area, but its importance wasn't always celebrated by Sanford. It includes the final resting place of Drew Bundini Brown, a corner man for Muhammad Ali who helped craft some of the boxer's most famous taunts. There is also an unused plot for Zora Neale Hurston. The land was donated by a local man, William Page-Jackson, who was either a gravedigger or a local farmer who allowed people to be buried there for free and who maintained the property.

Page-Jackson's story is another local legend that adds to the overall history of the place. People say that after he passed away, the care of the land never officially switched over to anyone else, and the property fell into disrepair. Unlike the other cemeteries that make up Evergreen, the city does not contribute to the maintenance. Many of the graves are sunken into the ground or sprayed with graffiti, and the forest has claimed much of the land back, until recent times, when local organizers have made a strong effort to save the site. People who volunteer to clean it up find links to past African Americans in the area. A sense of reverence for the place now exists that had not been present for a long time. Unfortunately, some larger family plots look as though grave robbers had their way with them and broke the fences and barriers down on their way in.

It was not until more people went in to take care of the place that stories of hauntings began to come out. Whether something has been awakened on the land or the presence of more people means more exposure, people are now talking about seeing things they can't explain. Paranormal investigators and cemetery enthusiasts who go there at night now consider it one of the most active places in Central Florida. Almost all of the reports are nonspecific and mundane. People have seen shadows or heard crying at night. The nature and tone of these are so broad that one wonders if there is anything there or if people just feel there needs to be.

This is not where the Lady of Shiloh is seen, though. Behind Page-Jackson is yet another, even older cemetery in even worse shape. In addition, it lacks the gravity of being an important historic location. This means that fewer people know about it and even fewer care for or visit it. It is often mentioned as the sister cemetery to Page-Jackson, to the point that some of the ghosts seen there are said to belong to the latter and have wandered into Shiloh for some reason. When you've reached the back of Page-Jackson, and after you've taken a few moments to think about why we would ever let our dead be treated so disrespectfully, you'll see a dirt road that leads to something even more heartbreaking and frightening. Maybe this is why there is such a dark feeling there. The dead seem to know they are not cared for.

The first thing you'll notice is an immediate shift in the atmosphere. You'll start to feel as if eyes are on you, even during the day, and then you'll notice that you can't hear anything. There are no birds or planes overhead. Normally, you're far from the traffic of the street, but there is always that little hum of distant cars. Not in Shiloh. There, you feel in a bubble, and when the growls and voices from the woods start, you feel as if you're trapped inside with something. Dark shadows are seen there at night, but there have been even more frightening sightings during the day. Drew tells a story in which a large shadow mirrored her as she walked among the headstones. When she took a step, it took a step. When she moved toward the woods, it moved to intercept her. "I was so scared but also didn't fully understand what was happening. I think about it now, and I wonder why I didn't just take off. But I was almost hypnotized by him." It wasn't until she grabbed her phone to take a picture that the shadow disappeared. "No, it didn't just vanish, it sank into the ground."

Listen to enough stories, and a pattern starts to emerge. Women have a particularly spooky time at Shiloh. Whatever is there takes a particular interest in them. Women have said they feel as though they are being watched or have the sensation of being touched, something no men have reported. Paranormal researchers have got voices on tape that describe the females in extremely misogynistic and crude ways. The same recordings contain a low and gravelly voice talking sweetly to the women, using terms of endearment and inviting them to come into the woods. This has led some to believe that a serial killer may have used the area to hunt or dispose of bodies.

The legends surrounding the Lady of Shiloh now reflect that aspect, giving her a story that draws people in and offers some of the biggest questions. According to the website BackPackerVerse, a psychic made contact with the spirit a number of years ago and was able to get a bit of its history. According to the man, the woman was murdered by a serial killer about twenty years earlier (the article is not specific regarding the period the man is speaking about) and dumped in a body of water nearby. The fish ate off her skin, and now she is doomed to stay in Shiloh.

With so many missing people and murders reported in the area, the tale does not seem that far-fetched, and several serial killers used this part of Florida as a hunting ground. A likely candidate for the spirit is April Marie Stone, whose body was found by the side of the road in 1991. The young woman was found stabbed to death and wrapped in a blanket on Painted Post Road near the Wekiva River, more than ten miles away from Shiloh. Accused serial killer William Devin Howell was thought to be responsible for her death but has never been formally charged. The primary problem with this theory is that Stone was known for her long red hair, and all the news reports from the time mention it. If the spirit in Shiloh had red hair, it seems likely that detail would be offered up. It is possible that nighttime sightings make it difficult to determine the spirit's hair color.

The legend itself has changed, however, based on Stone's murder. Late in 2017, the Stone theory made the rounds—the ghost could possibly

Another place where the skeleton ghost is seen.

be of the local redhead. The internet began to shift, too. Websites that discuss the spirit in the cemetery now include comments from witnesses and people who have been following the legend that report the spirit as having flowing red hair.

There are, of course, problems with all of this, not the least of which is that the information was given by a psychic who never determined the woman's name or her connection to that specific location. Saying someone died in a body of water is like saying someone died near an oak tree; there are just too many to make the place specific enough to use. In addition, the time frame fits into classic motifs for urban legends and folklore. Twenty years is just enough time for it to seem plausible but not specific enough to do any real research into it. That's the beauty of the Lady of Shiloh, though. There is enough information for you to hit the internet and think you might have found who the suspect is.

Here's the thing, though. The Lady of Shiloh is not like other ghosts, or at least she varies enough that her sightings have the feel of genuine encounters. Her half-eaten face or skeleton face is not often a detail attributed to ghost stories. In cases where this is reported, the ghost is usually said to be angry or even violent toward people. She doesn't fit that description, which leads people in the area who have not seen her to think she must be real. Perhaps the stories that have been used to flesh out her appearance are works of fiction. But there is someone there, lonely, wandering and seemingly trapped.

9
THE DARK MAN OF THE OCALA

There are unexplained things even in the world of the unexplained. While no one can really provide answers for all the weird things outside the lines, some phenomena have appeared to people for so long and have been looked at by so many people that there has been time to classify them. Ghost lights, for example, might be natural or supernatural, but they are such a part of the paranormal landscape that those who spend time studying them can offer theories that make sense or provide a level of understanding. There are, however, phantoms that defy explanation but pop up when people share stories or talk about legends. Their appearance is usually cyclical, brought up by television shows and ghost books. People look back on their experiences, and something clicks. Other phenomena have always been there, but because they do not conform to what the witness understands about the paranormal, they are dismissed. Maybe there is a whisper to a friend, just enough information to see if someone else has experienced the same thing. But for the most part, these experiences get pushed back into the dark spaces of memory until someone else comes forward.

The Dark Man is one such character, and constant appearances of these men in the Ocala and surrounding towns add an element of confusion and terror to the big picture. Visitors almost expect to see weird people or even ghosts, but when these dark figures make themselves known, it inspires a different level of fear. There are some theories as to what these men are. Some feel they are just any other ghosts but for some reason look different than a standard specter. Others add a little folklore and attribute their darkness to something evil they may have done in life—a walking curse reflecting the shadowy person they were in life.

Others, observing that the dark figures are reported as thick shadows with no features, call them demons or elementals. The fact that they are much more likely to be seen in places where other supernatural things have been seen adds some weight to this. They seem to be watchers, witnessing the activity and people's reaction to it, maybe even feeding on it. Another breed of these men wears hats, conjuring thoughts of transdimensional creatures, maybe even shadows of us from another place or time.

I first came across them when gathering stories from my students who had been tormented by them while serving time in a converted mental health facility in Massachusetts. These were juvenile criminals and not entirely trustworthy, but I recorded dozens of the reports over the course of five years from kids who had never met each other but who suffered from the same experience. It continued as I looked into Pukwudgies, a mythical creature that people were still sighting and one often accompanied by these dark men. Then I moved to Florida and took reports of them in St. Petersburg,

One of the places in the Ocala where the Dark Man is seen. *Courtesy of Heather Whiteman.*

where we were stalked by one while we were looking for the Mini-Lights and ran into another one while we waited in a cemetery to see the Ghost Pants of Holiday. Then there was Safety Harbor, the Devil's Tree in Port St. Lucie, Shiloh Cemetery in Sanford and Stetson University in Deland. When they are mentioned in relation to the Ocala, it is rarely in a nice context. In the forest, they are always considered more than a ghost and never friendly.

Haunted locations such as Tiger Trail Road in Dunnellon or the many streets of Astor have a bit more lore related to who the creepy men might be, but other places are left with just stories told in bits and pieces. According to author Kathleen Walls in her book *Finding Florida's Phantoms*, people have seen the Dark Man in the woods, sometimes lying down on paths and roads within the Ocala National Forest. Timothy reports spending time in several of the campsites inside the forest and sometimes waking up as a kid to see a strange Dark Man sitting and staring at the embers of the fire they had made. "Each one we went to. I used to wonder if he was following me, but I would ask other kids I ran into. You see the same people every year, but new people too. They said they saw him, too. He's always looking into the fire. I'm just staring at him through this little hole in my tent because I'm freaked out."

Heather had many odd experiences on her street in Silver Springs, most associated with a stretch they used to call Little Green Bridge. She and her mother are into the paranormal and have done research on sightings in their town and the Ocala. They came across reports of a man in a long trench coat and wearing a top hat but laughed them off. But then Heather herself saw the man. "I was driving home and saw a man appear out of nowhere in a black top hat and trench coat walking across the road. There are no streetlights on that road, so the only light was from my headlights. I thought it was really a man, and I slammed on my brakes, and in a blink of an eye he was gone." In the moment, she was concerned about hitting him, but looking back, she realizes the man did not come out of the woods or walk into the trees. He was just there in the middle of the road instantly and then vanished as soon as she should have hit him. "I looked all around and nothing was there. I remember thinking to myself when I first saw the man, 'What is he wearing? It's hot as hell out.'" Heather describes the man as being at least six feet tall and solid enough that she thought he was a real person.

Kimberly's experience took place in Gainesville, a little more than a half hour from the forest, but for some reason she connects the darkness in the forest with what happened to her. In early 2020, she found herself alone in

The street where Heather saw her Dark Man. *Courtesy of Heather Whiteman.*

her apartment because her boyfriend was in the hospital. She was not scared or nervous; she had lived alone often. She was a big fan of horror movies and documentaries and did not scare easily. "I woke to the sound of the coffee maker. Now [my boyfriend] is the only one who makes the coffee, and he wasn't home. Before I even opened my eyes, I felt a chill, because who or what would be making coffee in the middle of the night? When I opened my eyes, I saw a dark figure standing in the doorway." She immediately grew scared and felt what she describes as negative energy coming from whatever was there. "I couldn't make out much detail, but for some reason, I could feel that it was male. He had a hat on with a brim."

Almost immediately, the man was gone. She ran out to the kitchen to see if coffee had been made, but the machine was off and the pot was empty. She sat down in her living room, trying to make sense of what had happened. The Dark Man had definitely been threatening, but she was unsure as to why he chose to visit her and why that night. She eventually fell asleep, only to be awakened by a picture she had placed on a shelf being thrown six feet across the room. She tried to make sense of what happened but came up with no explanation of how it could have traveled that far, especially when nothing else around it had been disturbed. "After two hours of trying everything I could think of to try to make them fall, I gave up. I came to the conclusion that there was no way on our planet, our gravity, that what happened to those objects could naturally happen. You see, I really wanted to believe that somehow it could happen naturally. But it didn't, and then I was faced with the problem."

Kimberly felt she couldn't tell anyone what happened or ask for help. She eventually made her way to Otter and Trout, an herb shop in Gainesville. They suggested she use black sage to remove whatever it was and to protect her in the future. It seemed to help. She has not had another such experience and has no desire to go through anything like that again. She is now scared to stay anywhere overnight by herself or to be alone at night. "I will never sleep alone in the house again. There will always be that fear now. I don't think I can shake it." While Kimberly still does not know why it happened (she feels it had something to do with her boyfriend being in the hospital and may have even been a message), she recently read something about shadow men and feels she came face to face with one.

Then there is the bunker. Not far from Rodman Dam in Palatka, Florida, is a thick section of the Ocala that becomes swampy in the summer months but is broken up with thin roadways made of dark-orange sand. It's popular with local hikers and people who race four-wheelers and dirt bikes through the woods, because they can drive the path for miles, slip into the smaller, lesser-known trails among the trees and then emerge at campgrounds. The roads, like most in and around the forest, can only be identified by their numbers, so anyone unfamiliar with the area is taking a chance relying on their phone's GPS to find their way through.

Road 77 is one of several dirt roads that cut across the main path and leads back to County Road 315. Less than a mile from 315 is a bunker hidden about twenty-five yards into the woods. If you don't know what you're looking for, there is no way to find it, but those who have come across it spread the word about the odd structure and tell stories of something evil that may live there. The bunker itself has no history. Unlike some of the shelters in other parts of the forest, this one is small and not connected to bombing locations or military maneuvers. It is, however, made of thick concrete like the others. But unlike its possible brothers, it stands in a random location and is over seven feet high but only about ten feet long. If you can climb the moss-covered cement to the top, you'll find that the entire structure is closed with a hole, sticking out like a chimney that obviously used to have a cover. Take a rusty set of stairs, and you'll be another seven feet under the ground, knee-deep in murky water and staring into complete darkness.

Right: The road leading to the Bunker.

Below: The Bunker where the Dark Man is seen.

The bunker has taken on a life of its own, with explorers coming up with their own history or reason for its existence. Some say it has a military origin or was built by the Civilian Conservation Corps back in the day, which makes the most sense, given the number of these buildings the CCC actually did build in the area. Others point to the crudeness of it and claim it was built by biker gangs or cults to be used for sinister reasons. This does not make much sense, because it can be seen easier in the winter months and stands out in the woods because of its height. Criminals and cults in forests tend to build entirely underground. One person reported finding clothes small enough for a child and being told by his parents that kids went missing and were taken there and kept prisoner. While he took it as a story they told him to keep him away and to stress the dangers of the forest, the kidnapped children have become something of an urban legend in that part of the Ocala. The bunker can be found by geocachers who have marked it off and leave gifts and messages for one another there.

But other things find their way to the building. Allen was using his geocaching app to find it one day around dusk. He had already hit several locations near Rodman Dam, and this one was an afterthought. He only wanted to see it because he had heard it was spooky and a hideout for serial killers. He did not believe the stories but loved the idea of a concrete block in the middle of the woods. When he got there, the sun was setting quickly, so he almost missed it. "The app went completely out. I was pretty close, like a hundred feet, and it just wouldn't work anymore. I just started walking into the woods to the last location I got. It's a huge block of concrete in the middle of trees. It should have been easy to find." As he walked, he began to feel as if he were being watched. He remembers even snapping his head side to side to try to catch whatever it was. As he got closer to the bunker, he saw a dark figure run away from it. "It was still light out. Dark, but still light. This was like a shadow, but there shouldn't have been a shadow. I had my flashlight, just in case, and tried to follow him with it. He was gone." Allen looked for the geocaching artifact but couldn't find it. He estimates he spent about ten minutes there, and the entire time he kept seeing the same shadowy figure running through the woods nearby. He would appear in one place and then disappear and pop up in another place.

"I was about to give up. The thorns were too much, and I was hot and pretty scared. I turned the corner to start to go back to my car. He was just standing there in my way. No face, nothing. But I could tell he was staring at me." Allen brought his flashlight up, but the dark man was gone. He started to run back to the road, straight in the direction from which he had come.

A quick look inside the bunker.

He ran and ran, but for some reason he could not make it back to 77. "I started to pray. I asked to please help me out, and then there was the road." When he checked his watch, more than an hour had passed, although he was there for only about twenty-five minutes.

Barbara had an even scarier experience at the bunker. She admits having made a few wrong turns to get on the road, but she was on her way to meet her boyfriend to do a little mudding on the backroads. It was a little after midday, which is why it surprised her that a man should appear in the road out of nowhere. "I'm telling you, and you're going to think I'm crazy, but he was not there and then he was there." She admits that her mind was somewhere else but says there was no way he could have come out of the trees and into the middle of the road so quickly. She describes the man as looking more like a black bear. "It wasn't, though. I just mean it was this thick black color and was really tall. It was wearing like an old-time hat pushed down one side of its face." She immediately hit the brakes and skidded to a stop but felt as if she had hit whoever was standing there. When she got out, there were no footprints and no evidence anyone had been there.

That was when she heard what sounded like moans from the woods. "I wasn't driving fast, but I thought maybe I knocked him into the trees." She followed the sound, which she realized afterward kept coming from deeper in the woods. After a few minutes she came across the bunker. "I'm not sure how tall that thing is, but there was no ladder or anything. There is no way he could have gotten to the top that fast." Barbara says the figure was sitting cross-legged on the top, looking in her direction. "Except there were no eyes. It was just this black thing in the shape of a man with no face. It looked like it was wearing a cape or something and that hat. I don't think it was human." She ran back to her car and drove immediately home, making an excuse to her boyfriend as to why she never met him and telling no one about what happened until years later.

10

THE CURSE OF *JEEPERS CREEPERS*

Legend tripping came into popularity in the late 1940s, just as young people were gaining access to cars and driving on Saturday nights. The idea was not something new. People had been creeping into cemeteries and daring each other to knock on the town haunted house for generations, but the automobile allowed them the freedom to mix meeting up with friends with finding excuses to huddle close to a date in the hopes of getting them in the back seat. That was also about the time Dunnellon High School was built, but none of the drivers looking for ghosts parked along Tiger Trail Road, the informal name for 180th Road. Adventurous visitors searched for the mysterious figures said to walk the street late at night. Those ghosts, and the curse said to have given birth to them, are a modern invention.

Tiger Trail has a new legend trip, born in modern times, that changes as social media continues to refine it. On that stretch of road, another type of Dark Man walks across the street, waiting to be conjured by teens who know the ritual. You drive past the high school and park under the special tree (those in the know understand which one it has to be) and then turn off your lights. When you turn them back on, there will be a dark figure in the distance, barely visible except on moonlit nights. Turn your lights off and then back on, and he will be closer, standing still but clearly watching you in your car. Turn them off again, and he comes closer until he is so close that he can touch the hood of your car. You would be able to see his face now, if he had a face for you to see, but the only details you can make

The infamous view of "Poho County" from the movie *Jeepers Creepers*.

out are his bulky, seven-foot frame and the hat he wears slightly tipped to one side. If you dare to try one more round, when you turn the light on, he kills everyone in the car.

Unlike some ghost stories, there is a way to tempt fate and still come away alive. When you are turning your lights on and off, make sure that you're turning on the high beams. When he's as close as you want him, repeat the process but make sure your high beams are off and you're turning on low beams. He will start to move farther away until he is out of sight. Do it a few more times just to make sure, and you can continue your night and not worry about him following you home. If not, he will be seen all around you after you leave until you slowly go crazy.

This creepy road trip has developed over the last few years, its growth due to a few horror movies and urban legends developed on YouTube and TikTok. The unexplained people seen on the road, the ones who have inspired locals to attach these newer stories, date back a little bit longer, to 2001 and the release of the horror movie *Jeepers Creepers*. Movie curses are nothing new, from *The Omen* and *Poltergeist* to *The Crow* and *The Fast and the Furious*. Whenever tragedy surrounds a production or the unexplained follows the cast, people look to the paranormal for an explanation. In the case of *Jeepers Creepers*, residents of the towns used for filming report that the darkness surrounding the horror movie continues to scream out to them.

The urban legend of that story draws from an even older true crime that occurred 1,300 miles away in Michigan. On Easter 1990, Dennis DePue beat his wife, Marilyn, in front of their three children and left the house with her, telling them he was taking her to a nearby hospital. He instead shot her in the head and attempted to dump the body, wrapped in a bloody sheet, behind a nearby church. A random couple, the Thorntons, drove by the location just as he was hauling the body out of his van, but they were unsure of what they saw. DePue jumped in his van and followed the Thorntons, almost getting close enough to ram them, honking his horn and flashing his lights. The pursuit continued until Ray Thornton turned onto another road and DePue switched directions and went the other way. A year later, the case was featured on an episode of *Unsolved Mysteries*. Dennis DePue came out of hiding for the first time since the murder. He was eventually found and surrounded but committed suicide before the police could take him in.

The writer and director of *Jeepers Creepers*, Victor Salva, has come out saying that the DePue killing did not inspire his story, but the similarities are too eerie to dismiss. In the movie, two siblings are driving home from college to spend the holidays. They enter rural Poho County, filmed on Tiger Trail Road, and see a mysterious man dumping a body into a well chute. They slow down and catch a glimpse and rush off, only to have his car follow them, jamming them, honking its horn and flashing its lights. They lose him, but he continues to hunt them until they find out that it's a town monster that comes out every twenty-three years for twenty-three days. It eats as many people as it can, storing some for later and using human body parts to replace its own that have aged and died.

The movie was a hit, breaking records at the time of its release. The production of the movie was not without its problems. No one is sure if the curse caused the problems or if making the movie created something monstrous. In the paranormal world, there is something known as a *tulpa*, or a thought form. If we think about something long enough, we can create it, and it takes on a life of its own, like the Jewish golem.

Some believe it starts with Salva himself. In 1988, he was charged with the sexual abuse of a minor and possession of child pornography, including a recording he had made of the abuse. He pled guilty and served fifteen months. This led to trouble during the shooting of *Jeepers Creepers*, when Salva tried to employ high schoolers as extras in the film. He also insisted on filming in the shadow of the Ocala, something people warned him about. He found the setting ideal for his story. But insects, always an unwanted annoyance in Florida, were so bad that the crew had to fire off guns to scatter them before takes. Although the fake county of Poho is used in the film and almost all locations mentioned are made up, there are several references to Lady Lake, the home of several ghostly legends. The weirdest hiccup during filming stems from the White Meat Packing Plant location in the film. According to researcher and author David Goudsward, the final scene was filmed in the abandoned factory, which was in such horrible condition that little had to be done to dress it up for the shoot. Several members of the crew were so scared of the location that they refused to go inside and film; others who did reported suffering from horrible nightmares for nights afterward.

After the movie was released, the ghost stories started. One of the most common reports involve ghost children, usually three together, often holding hands. They glide across the street as shadows, unaware of the cars driving past them. Other people say they glow an eerie green and try to flag down cars or intentionally jump in front of moving vehicles in an attempt to get them to drive off the road. Confused by seeing the small children out at night, some people stop to try to help. The kids turn and stare at the driver and then lumber toward the car with blank, black eyes. The people drive off in fear before the children get to them. That is, if their cars will start. An aspect of the sightings are mysterious engine and cell phone mishaps on that part of the road. This almost always happens late at night or in the early morning, leading to the notion that the best time to see them is at 3:00 a.m., a time known as the witching hour, or the devil's hour. It is a new theme seen in horror movies and newer urban legends and ghost stories.

BackPackerVerse describes another type of sighting. A man on his way to work in the early morning reported a family of five, describing the "adults" as being teenagers and all of them as having deformed faces and black holes for eyes. On that website, they are even said to appear in the back seat of cars, bleeding from their mouths and eyes.

Some residents say the whole thing is a publicity stunt designed to promote the film and its sequel. While no one remembers the legend being told before 2001, one of the accidents said to be the reason for the children's appearances happened years before. It doesn't, however, make much sense to promote the movie years later, and it is not as if following up on the story brings money

Right: The road where all types of ghostly legends are seen.

Below: Dunnellon High School.

The cemetery where the real ghosts of *Jeepers Creepers* are seen.

or notoriety to the location. Another earthly explanation might involve the nearby high school. It makes more sense for the students there to be out at night in that area, especially after it was identified on different websites as a haunted location. Who would not want to go out and scare people for a good time? It is also worth noting that as the popularity of the location grew, the time to see the ghostly children changed to 3:00 a.m. Initial stories spoke of seeing them at dusk and around midnight, but as the story has become more popular, it has taken on the infamous time for hauntings.

Then there is the Dark Man with the hat. It is worth noting that this description is pretty close to what the killer in *Jeepers Creepers* looks like, so it makes sense that people could misidentify what they have seen or that the Dark Man might be a hoax being conducted by locals aware of the popularity of the spot with fans of the film.

The curse does not end there. Follow State Road 40 into Ocala, and you'll eventually come to the old St. James Church, which was used in the abandoned church scenes in the movie. It has been said to be the scene of ghostly activities well before the movie was shot there, and it continues to be frequented by thrill seekers and paranormal enthusiasts. People have said that an unexplained fog rolls in unexpectedly and that weird noises, especially scratching and moaning, can be heard near the church and adjacent cemetery. Odd lights and orbs appear in the windows of the church, and dark figures are spotted among the headstones, sometimes appearing to bury someone—similar to the actions of the bad guy in the movie.

The problem is that the church no longer exists. After the movie came out, local teens were known to hang out and party there. It became an eyesore and a sensitive topic for the community, and it was scheduled to be torn down. According to David Goudsward, before that could happen, an arsonist burned the church down in 2003. A local paranormal group, the Paranormal and Ghost Society, offers an explanation for the ghostly legend. According to its website, another nearby church is the actual location for some of the hauntings attributed to St. James. They have reported activity there, much of it similar to the stories coming from the *Jeepers Creepers* location. Wesley Chapel United Methodist Church, which suffered one of those mysterious fires in 1967 that this part of Florida is famous for in its haunted locations, now looks like a new church, but the graves still date to the 1800s.

11

THE LADY IS STILL WALKING

J ulia was murdered. If the residents of Lady Lake can't agree on the exact details of the ghostly woman they see on Rolling Acres Road, they all agree that she was killed. The particulars depend on the people who tell you the legends and who they heard it from. Julia was in love; most people can agree on that as well. Beyond that, the details get muddied and borrowed and adjusted to when people think she may have died. Most say she died of a gunshot wound to the heart, which created a bloodstain on her white dress. No matter what people see or claim to see on that stretch of road or what they hear from a friend, everyone agrees that, no matter where else she can be seen in the town, Julia walks the road.

The most popular story involves a love triangle. Julia had fallen in love with a man whom her parents did not approve of. The couple would walk Rolling Acres together, making plans for the future and making sure no one was looking when they kissed. Her parents, determined to find a better man for her, set her up with someone of high social standing, a man who would lift her and their family name. But she had no romantic feelings for him. One night, Julia's parents invited him over for dinner, but the man she really loved snuck over uninvited and viewed them through the window. Determined that she should be with no one but him, he went home and got his gun. When she went out to meet him later that night, he shot her dead before killing himself.

Other versions have the man she loved dying in a war. She goes out into the street in the wedding dress she was to be married in and shoots herself in

The place where Julia walks.

the heart. One version has him going off to war and her parents taking that opportunity to set her up with a more proper husband. The veteran comes home, kills her and commits suicide.

Julia is very real to the people of Lady Lake. She is seen dressed all in white—some people take it to be a wedding dress—walking toward the dead end of the road. She does not talk to anyone, even those who stop and ask her if she is OK or needs a ride home. While some roadside ghosts get into the car, Julia keeps walking. "My father said she was ignoring him," says Ben, who retells a story his late father told him about his experience. "It was not as if she couldn't hear him. Some ghosts are like that, they say. They are just a replay. He said it wasn't like that. She put her chin in the air and was crying. Then my dad said she disappeared, and he didn't tell anyone. He didn't drink or anything, but he had been working like crazy and thought he had imagined it. He told my mom and I, and it wasn't until people started talking about it online that I made the link."

That sounds similar to other people's experiences, even if most people of Lady Lake consider the story nothing more than an urban legend and a nuisance.

Florida is littered with the skeletons of small towns that share a similar history, and nowhere is this more apparent than in those scattered around the Ocala Forest. A homestead is carved out of the woods or the swamp, and other people come and settle there. People arrive to take advantage of the natural resources or something unique in the area, and a small boom occurs, drawing in even more people. Then, usually without fanfare or anything overwhelming to point to, the town fails. Frost or fire or disease can sometimes be to blame, but often the demise of the town is more a whimper than a bang. Many times, the government comes in and takes over the land, or a big company buys it up and plants acres of a crop, in which case, passing through feels more like driving among the rows of a citrus grove. In the worst scenario, the traditions of the town, along with its ghost stories, are erased. Other times, the town can reinvent itself, taking the old stories along for the ride and changing them if needed.

Lady Lake suffers from a lost sense of self. It's one part Leesburg, a town with a rich history and a rich paranormal center, and one part The Villages, the relatively new community not without its own issues and controversy. Lady Lake prides itself on being known as the "Gateway to The Villages," but its past goes back much further than that. It was a railroad town incorporated in 1885 in the shadow of the Seminole Wars and the Homestead Act of 1862. Like its neighbors, it prospered under the conditions of Central Florida following the Civil War, although it did not suffer many of the setbacks of its neighbors. It was able to cling tight enough during its down years to survive until the time when it could flourish again. You might not even realize you've entered another town if it wasn't for the signs welcoming you. The main streets are primed by commerce, with franchises on either side of the road broken up by parks and playgrounds. If you know where you are, it feels like the foyer of The Villages. Get off the main streets, and you'll find a more rural setting with ranches and long driveways. It is here that the urban legends and ghost stories take hold.

The oldest and perhaps the oddest is told about the naming of the town itself, and the story hints that there may have been something supernatural happening before it was settled by Europeans. Boomtowns were usually named for their first citizens or the politicians and businessmen crucial to their development. Either that, or people fell back on a Native American name they had grown used to using, often adopted from a local body of water. Lady Lake follows this, in a way, although it owes more to the legend surrounding the water than to the lake itself. According to Seminoles in the area, years ago, a settler woman had been found mysteriously drowned in the lake. Some say she continued to haunt the location. As a way of appeasing her, they named it after her. Or maybe the designation was just to remind people that there was something off about the place. Either way, the newly formed town borrowed what the Seminoles had started and simply called the new town Lady Lake.

Julia is an old story pasted on the new landscape, a possible memory of the past or a new story trying to explain away a woman who talks at night and disappears without a word. But there is more to her. If you listen to the stories of the people from Lady Lake, she may be the woman they see at the foot of their beds and in their kitchens late at night. For a Woman in White, she has a habit of getting around. This mirrors the Ocala Syndrome felt by many in Central Florida. Julia is a ghost that people expect to see, so they cast her in all the things in town that send chills down their spines. But it might be a different boogeyman, one with a dark history in the area, that's truly to blame for her death and her haunting.

For as long as anyone can remember—long enough that her last name is lost to records and tax rolls—the ghost of the young lover has been seen walking the road, trying to get home. She never makes it. Just about every town has a legend involving picking up a hitchhiker who disappears when approached, but the people of Lady Lake say this one has really happened to them. Victor, a resident who has driven the road for several years but had never heard the story, tried to see if a female pedestrian was OK one night in 2018. "Now I hear the stories, and I found it on different sites. Not when I saw her. She was leaning on one of the rails and looked sick. It was late, so I stopped right in front of her to check on her. I turned the radio down, and she was gone. It was like a second, and she was in a dress. She couldn't have taken off without me seeing it."

Different rituals have developed around the ghost. They say if you drive to the intersection of Rolling Acres Road and Lake Ella Road and turn off your car, you can catch the ghost. Roll your windows down, and you'll hear voices in the woods. This may be the voice of Julia, but others say it is a female child crying out for help or calling for her father. If you honk your horn three times, something will tap on your window. There is a

Park by the fence, shut off your lights and see if you can hear the screams on Rolling Acres Road.

warning, though. People who attempt to contact her this way suffer from unexplained engine failure and have trouble leaving. In fact, many people say their cars break down in this part of town for no reason and attribute it to the ghost of Julia.

There is more to the story. The woods surrounding the road, especially on the western side, where the pavement disappears and the road abruptly stops at a dead end, is said to be haunted. Then there are the more recent reports of a mysterious Dark Man in the road, sometimes described as looking like the Grim Reaper. He's a fairly new addition to the story, and it is reasonable to assume it could be the influence of this man seen all around the Ocala Forest that has added him as a character in Lady Lake. Children are heard crying from the trees in the dark, and some residents have even reported hearing unhuman growls and screams. BackPackerVerse even tells of drivers reporting three ghostly children. They are reported to appear in the back seats of cars driving the Rolling Acres late at night. In one story, the kids are seen as if they had been involved in an accident, with blood coming from their noses and mouths. These experiences may or may not be true, but they add to the hysteria surrounding the haunting.

That hysteria, mixed with the idea of the Ocala Syndrome, affects the town. It includes a belief in Julia so deep that she gets blamed for everything. Lady Lake is a haunted town, even though there is little evidence that it has seen the tragedies and had the history of other towns. People report several ghosts for such a small community, and when their minds try to wrap around what they have seen, they fall back on the Woman in White to explain it away, even if the spirit they see is not wearing white. Time and again, people online connect a ghost they see in their kitchen, living room or barn to Julia. No strong description of her face exists, so she makes for a great canvas on which stories can be told. Even those who disagree with the legend will go on to tell their own ghost story and talk about how traffic in the area has made it less likely to see her but that their friend might have seen her at the kitchen table, wringing her hands. This helps to keep her alive. These random connections add to her lore and justify what people see on the road, an instance of one hand washing the other. She gives you a platform for understanding but also a forum to talk about what has happened to you. In a small town, you might never share a true ghost story, but if people are already spinning tales of the Woman in White, you can get the story out without fear of being laughed at.

Another theory might explain the ghost and the other oddness that has grown around it. In 2007, a murder case was officially closed, even though no charges were filed and no murderer was brought to justice. The full story of Pamela Nater and Nancy Leichner might never be known, but police are satisfied that they know who abducted and killed the two women.

In October 1966, Nater and Leichner, relative strangers but part of a skin-diving club known as the Aquaholics, walked down a nature trail in the Alexander Springs Recreation Center in Altoona. They were never seen again. They left their purses and personal belongings on a picnic bench, implying that whatever they were planning to do did not involve leaving the park or straying too far. Both of the men who had come to the park with them later said the women were good swimmers. (One wouldn't join a skin-diving club if one wasn't.) But they also said that the water was too cold that day to make diving possible. No trace was ever found of the women. Of the few suspects the police considered, none was a sufficient match for the perpetrator of the crime. It was not until later that it became clear from evidence and motive who the killer was.

If Florida has a boogeyman, his name is Gerard John Schaefer, who became a deputy in the early 1970s in Martin County. He may be Florida's most prolific serial killer. He claimed to have killed dozens of women during his active hunting time. In addition to potentially being connected to the redheaded ghost of Shiloh Cemetery, his name is spoken of often in Oak Hammock Park in Port St. Lucie. Most people know the park by its other feature, as the home of the Devil's Tree. It is said that Schaefer killed two women at the location and left their bodies to hang from a tree there, although the bodies were found a distance away and not in or under a tree, as legend tells. That location is one of the darkest in Florida, said to be the home not only of Schaefer's ghost but also of the ghost of the women who now haunt the bathroom there. The whole park is said to be cursed. The tree has proven indestructible over the years. Anyone who tries to or takes bark or a branch from the tree is said to take that curse home. The woods are said to now be home to a cult that comes together to worship the serial killer and praise the evil spirits that make the park their home. These may be rumors, but it proves the kind of stories that are inspired by the man.

The story of Nater and Leichner is no exception. Schaefer was known to be drawn toward pairs of women, and the murders he was convicted of in October 1973 are eerily similar to the abduction of the women in Altoona. Before the trial, his mother's house was searched. Evidence was found that implicated him in several other double murders across the state. Although he never confessed to being involved in Nater and Leichner's deaths (he was known to lie and brag about his involvement in murders), evidence and statements from another convict were enough to have the police close the case.

Altoona is more than twenty miles from Lady Lake, so it may be hard to connect the murder of these women to Julia and what people see on Rolling Acres. However, there was evidence in 1966 and 1967 that Schaefer may have transported the bodies to Lady Lake after they were abducted. He almost always traveled with the women he took to a second location, and it would not have made sense to stay in a crowded park once they were discovered missing. Whatever tips the police received at the time, before they knew about Schaefer, they searched the water in Lady Lake with boats and divers, believing the women could have been brought there.

The cries of "help" and "papa" from the woods also make sense in light of the Schaefer case. He often held victims for a time, physically and psychologically torturing them before leaving them. He often returned after their deaths. Several other hauntings are attributed to Schaefer in Florida, most notably the Devil's Tree in Port St. Lucie. Witnesses at these locations report a large, dark figure that appears to linger at the spot, just like at Rolling Acres. The notorious serial killer may be responsible for other murders in the Ocala Forest, where this same Grim Reaper has been reported for decades.

We want an easy way to explain it all away. That may seem like a contradiction: an easily explained ghost sighting. There are too many things we can't push aside as imagination or hallucination, so our mind is forced to consider that ghosts might exist. When we get there, we want it all to make sense and have the loose ends tied up. In the confusion, a haunting like the one happening on Rolling Acres Road makes more sense to us if we have the right story to go along with it. We say that ghosts aren't real—but if they are, they better come in a neat, familiar package. Lady Lake has that, and if we are still left trying to classify and understand all that happens on that dark road, the residents can at least find comfort in being able to tell a ghost story people can nod along with. As long as they do, Julia will continue to walk.

12
THE CRISSCROSS HAUNTING
OF DELTONA

The announcements come on, just like on every other day. The high
schoolers are half paying attention, most too consumed by their
earpods and phones or the pretty girl or handsome boy next to them
to even care what the administration is purring on about. It's the same old
thing: sports scores, yearbook deadlines and room changes for the Florida
State Assessments. It's the daily drone, but the few awake enough to listen
notice the other voice underneath. Only some of them can hear it, but it is
the unmistakable sound of someone crying, the sobs that come from pain
and the understanding that no one is coming to take it away. Just as the teens
strain to listen better, the other voice is gone in time for the announcement
of the lunch menu for tomorrow.

That's a typical day at Pine Ridge High School, if there can be a typical
day when your campus is haunted. It's something some students live with
and others never pick up on. Most who have been spreading the story since
the school opened point to the nameless worker who lost his life building
the school, but those in the town know that the roots run a bit deeper
and may go back to tainted ground dug out when the town was still being
built. The people who founded it set one section aside for a purpose other
than education.

Since its opening in 1994, the campus has been home to a persistent
rumor of ghostly activity. It seems that no school is complete without its
resident ghost, but at Pine Ridge, the story is a tradition passed on from

Pine Ridge High School.

student to student and staff member to staff member for over twenty-five years. Most of the activity is centered on the clock tower in the middle of campus. The bells used to signal the change of classes have a distinct sound. Students often hear another bell, lower and lasting longer. It goes mostly unnoticed but happens enough to keep the story going. Some chalked this up to malfunction, but a cause has never been found, and not everyone hears the phantom bell at the same time. A type of mass hysteria may be at work. Hearing the mystery bells is part of becoming a Panther. People hear it or say they hear it because it's part of the culture.

Of course, that area is no stranger to the idea of a haunted tower or ghostly bells. Less than fifteen miles away is Deland and Stetson University, home of Hulley Tower. Once measuring over one hundred feet tall, the base houses the mausoleum, which is the final resting place of Lincoln and Eloise Hulley, two of the founders of the university. Lincoln had hoped the building would become the center of the campus, a place for students to easily find one another and meet while on campus, but also a place to house the bells, which were originally part of a Methodist church in Pennsylvania. The bells would ring out the day and for important events. Eloise was in love

Left: Hulley Tower on the campus of Stetson University.

Right: One of Eloise's bells, and another haunted location on campus.

with the sound of them, and the construction of Hulley Tower was in part to make her happy. Lincoln died in 1934, just before the tower was completed. Eloise died a few decades later, in 1959. The couple may have found each other in death.

After Eloise died, the bells continued. The student who rang the bells was well trained and benefited from the honor of being part of the great tradition. It became common for them to feel hands on their shoulders and to feel an unexplained presence rush past them as they climbed the stairs. Several even saw Eloise in the tower, an experience that was echoed by other students who spotted her from the outside, usually at dusk. Most of them got into the habit of saying hello to the couple when they entered the building. At times, the bells went off even when no one was there to activate them. When the majority of the tower was taken down in 2005, people continued to hear the bells. Also, areas on campus that now house some of the original eleven bells, including the library and Elizabeth Hall, have their own ghost stories. The most endearing haunt associated with Hulley Tower places the couple on the lawn near it. The ghosts of Lincoln and Eloise are seen walking hand in hand in the early-morning hours before the majority of the students are up and the campus comes alive.

The ghost story associated with the tower at Pine Ridge High School is not quite the same pleasant love story. The legend tells of a worker who was horribly crushed while building the tower and who then died on campus before an ambulance could arrive. His spirit is now trapped and trying to communicate. He is one of two men said to have died at the school during its construction, although no record of either accident can be found.

The story remains, though, and the ghost is not confined to the clock. A dark figure has been seen walking the halls in the connected buildings. It is more than a shadow but less than an actual person, and it darts out of the way when people try to talk to it or walk after it. Teachers and students have reported things randomly falling or being thrown across classrooms in those buildings. Things are also misplaced, only to be found moments later in a place that had already been checked. The elevator, open only to staff and students in need, malfunctions and is said to experience severe temperature drops. Some have even said it will open when no one has called it. Similar cold spots happen around campus, along with the feeling of being watched. There is even a woman who whispers just low enough to not be understood.

Of course, all this activity happens when there are few people around to confirm anything, but it does create an atmosphere in which these stories spread and things that might have been natural experiences are assumed to be the product of the ghost. If you ask different people, you will get different reasons for the creepy happenings at the school. The most well known might be the man who died during construction, but another reason lies only a few hundred yards away. Some say that distance is much closer.

It starts with a case of vanished history and a lost cemetery that really isn't lost at all—it's just a little hidden behind a wall of progress. Take Osteen Cemetery Road past the new development, and you'll find Osteen Cemetery, a place where cell phones stop working and odd ghosts are seen. They say the cemetery's oldest burial took place in 1881, when M.F. and Annie Osteen buried an infant child. But look around at some of the worn headstones and listen to rumors of unmarked graves and rotted wood monuments, and you'll get a different story. Either way, the burial ground is inconvenient to outsiders who don't know what to look for, but it remains an active cemetery still frequented by mourners and still used to trace tragedy in the town.

Locals say the cemetery was started by the Osteen family, which made its money in cattle and then the railroads. They were vital to the development of Volusia County. In addition to the town of Osteen itself, you can trace their importance in business and street names while traveling through most of the area. There is also a bit of lost history. The town was originally

Osteen Cemetery comes right up to the new development.

known as Saulsville, after George Saul, one of the original settlers on the land. He moved there with his wife, Adeline, in the mid-1800s. He and his family became intertwined with the Osteens, even going so far as to pool their money to educate their kids together. Both families prospered when the stagecoach line came through, but that changed when transportation shifted to the railroads, which steered away from the area for stops a little to the east and west.

Both families suffered from the change, but the cemetery is a reminder of their standing in the town. Some sections are immaculate, with fancy headstones adorned with elaborate elegies; other parts look as though someone dug up a few mud-covered rocks and then gave up halfway through.

People often hear the crushing of leaves while visiting their loved ones. The footsteps are said to follow the people, stopping when they do. There is even the sound of someone running away and a strange feeling of being watched. A phantom mourner is said to put his hand on your shoulder when you stop by graves in the older part of the cemetery. People describe the feeling as if someone is trying to comfort you rather than scare you, and those who frequent Osteen know it well enough to not be scared. There are also reports of moaning, like a man suffering or experiencing immense pain.

This ghost might have another backstory, however. In 2013, James Sheaffer was lured to the location by a friend, Angela Stoldt. The two had a rocky relationship but shared a bank account and were said to be fighting over finances. Once there, Stoldt stabbed Sheaffer in the eye with an ice pick before strangling him with a rope. She then wrapped his head in plastic, brought his body home and chopped it up in a kiddie pool. She then tried to boil some parts on the stove and cremate others in her oven. Stoldt then returned to the cemetery to bury the parts. However, after she was caught and revealed the spots, authorities found no head. No one can remember when the moaning started, but they assume it's Sheaffer.

These stories are typical of any cemetery, but there is something that sets Osteen apart from others, There is a whispering of the other history of the town that people hate to talk about. For reasons no one can quite explain, Osteen unofficially extends past the new development and into the parking lot and athletic fields of Pine Ridge. There are no markers or death records. There are just stories of bodies disturbed and souls confused about what is going on. According to a plaque dedicated to the Sauls in 2006, "In 1884, Saul family members denoted this burial ground, along with an African American graveyard to the west." The school, it seems, was built over the final resting place of the forgotten in Volusia County.

There is no way to confirm this. The immense groves needed people to work them, and the hundreds of slaves who died in those years never got headstones or memorials. Nothing has ever been proven about this, but it is something the locals say as fact. As the town has grown, much of this land has been developed, leaving the final resting places in question. They are most likely underneath some of the new buildings. Records are hard to come by, and no one quite remembers there ever being headstones there. There has been no rush to check the ground or search dusty records to give them names or claim ownership of the land. Was there a large slave

Left: The site where the murder of James Sheaffer is said to have happened.

Below: Some of the older headstones at Osteen Cemetery.

or African American population in the area before the Civil War? One of the oddest things is the plaque's referencing a graveyard. It might be a case of semantics, but the difference between a cemetery and a graveyard is the presence of a church, and there are no records of a church on that land.

But there are still stories. Unknown men are seen on the field. They disappear or walk among the cars in the parking lot before vanishing. Mourners in the cemetery tell stories of wisps of smoke lingering along the fence of the new development before dissolving into the ground, as if someone is trying to get back to their grave, struggles with the boundary and then just goes under it.

Then there is the Whistling Man. The most talked-about ghost is one no one ever sees or feels. Instead, there is just a whistling that comes from the area near the wall separating the burial area from the new development. Some say it's a sad, somber song; others say it has a more upbeat feel to it. But all describe it as coming from a man. People split over who the man might be. Some say the songs are old hymns and connect it to the lost graves of the rumored slaves. Some claim that the ghost is the spirit of an unnamed man who lost his life down the street in an accident.

Crisscross hauntings are like that, which is why so many of the stories sound the same and so many are easy to believe. The ghosts in the cemetery are from the school. The ghosts from the school are from the cemetery. The man who died was pushed by the unsettled spirits from down the street. Angela Stoldt killed her friend because the voices from the hidden graveyard told her to. The stories shift, depending on where exactly you sit down in front of the campfire to hear the story.

13

A Famous Ghost
and a Famous Cemetery

The saying goes in the ghost world that a place is always haunted by the most famous person associated with it. That makes the story more relatable. Every place where George Washington ate or stepped is haunted by America's first president. Stephen Crane has to be one of the ghosts haunting Lilian Place in Daytona, and serial killer Gerard John Schaefer haunts everywhere he is rumored to have killed. It allows someone hearing the story to link the unknown to something they do know. This makes the tale feel more reasonable. The Ocala is no different.

Take for instance the weird lights seen in the sky and phantom planes reported in Leesburg. Ghost planes are not uncommon near the Ocala. For years, the government ran test-bombing missions above the woods, even allowing pilots from Israel to use its airspace. For decades, it has been one of the most written-about places in the state for UFO sightings. Most residents believe the lights in the sky and the mysterious planes that seem to appear and disappear are nothing more than secret craft being tested for another black operations mission. One persistent plane, seen by multiple people over the years, may be more ghostly legend than government conspiracy theory.

On March 19, 1982, Ozzy Osbourne's bus started to suffer from a broken air conditioner during the southern leg of the singer's American tour. The band had been traveling for most of the day, so they decided to stop at Flying Baron Estates in Leesburg to try to fix the problem and get some sleep. The Flying Baron was connected to the tour bus company, so the band was welcomed in. The bus driver, Andrew Aycock, was also

The site of the Randy Rhodes accident.

a pilot, and he decided to take one of the planes out despite having spent the downtime drinking and doing cocaine. When he finally got guitarist Randy Rhodes on the plane, he decided to buzz the tour bus as a joke. He clipped the wing on the vehicle, tipped the plane and crashed into the trees before slamming through the garage of the house. Rhodes and two others on the plane died on impact and were burned so badly they needed to be identified by dental records.

Since then, there have been several reports of ghost fires at the landing area and times when the accident replays itself. In all honesty, Leesburg, for being a small town, is a place where aircraft activity is common. Unlike at major airports, smaller planes have more erratic flight schedules and tend to appear and disappear easier on a cloudy day. Most people have never heard a plane crash, so seeing a plane vanish and then hearing a loud noise makes the mind relate the two. And just how far does the sound of a low-flying plane travel?

Common sense doesn't make the experience any less impactful for those who feel they know what happened. Daniel went out to ranches surrounding the Flying Baron one year on the anniversary of the crash. He and a few of his friends parked at one of the nearby ranches about two hundred yards from the airport and with a clear view of the historic spot. They arrived around dusk and waited to see something. "I know it didn't happen at night. To us it made sense to be there at nighttime, but we didn't want to be out there too late. I've heard ghosts are like animals; they come out at dawn and dusk." They brought along a small radio to play Randy Rhodes's music, and the three of them told ghost stories and looked to the skies.

After about twenty minutes, they heard a plane. "There were no clouds at all. I feel like we could see for miles and miles, but there was nothing there." He said the sound of the plane grew louder, as if it were overhead. They all heard it and looked across the field to the Flying Baron. "For maybe three seconds, I saw a plane pop out of nowhere and hit the ground. It didn't sound like it was hitting the ground, like the airplane noise didn't change. My buddies didn't see it, but the ground shook. It actually shook, and they felt that." He claims all three of them experienced a brief moment when they felt a shockwave, as if something had hit the ground near them, and then the airplane noise stopped.

No one as famous as Randy Rhodes died in the town of Umatilla, about twenty miles from the crash site. Instead, it is very much like the other small towns that dot the landscape around the Ocala, with a population that hovers around four thousand people. The town was founded in 1856. There has not been much to put the small town on the map in the past 150 years except the ghost stories people tell. There is a deep pride in the history of Umatilla among its citizens, but they often equate where they live in the town in relation to the Umatilla Cemetery, which is often listed as one of the most haunted places in Florida. They tell about the odd things that happen to them in town in relation to the burial ground, as if something about those headstones and the surrounding forest sets the stage for the experiences they have in their own homes. A phantom lumberjack seen in town, understood to be the product of an entirely made-up story, and the ghost of a Native American woman who walks in and out of shops in town, are said to have their origins in the cemetery. It's the kind of place where any story gains traction because so many people have driven by the boneyard at night and had their own experiences. Just about anything is possible.

The cemetery is split into two sections by Golden Gem Road, with most residents agreeing that the older section, which meanders off into citrus lands marked up by off-road vehicle tracks, is where the ghosts tend to be seen. Many times, there is nothing specific to point to. People just get an uneasy feeling there, even if they are just waking by. They can't quite explain it in words or speak about it in detail; there is just something off. According to Taylor McCall, who visits there most days to take care of the grounds and visit with different graves that tend to be neglected, everyone in town has a story. "People have walked by here and seen shadows. It's spooky at night. Maybe they [the ghosts] are unsettled. There's quite a bit about this town that people don't talk about, like secrets or things in the past we don't look

Umatilla Cemetery.

at too close. I think that's what's going on here. They were not ready to go. They want something to be known."

Other people who research it are less sure about why the place is so haunted. Toni Ray-Land, who used to research and write for the website Florida Fringe Tourism, points at the unknown history as part of the reason the spirits may be so disturbed. She writes that no one can quite point to when the cemetery came into being. There are clearly people buried there who fought for the Confederacy during the Civil War, and the older section has headstones dating back even further, yet records show the first burials to be in 1956. That may be just the thing that causes the uneasiness. History, even the dark kind that people want to hide, has a tendency to want to be remembered. Maybe the ghosts are a reminder to look through the whole story of the town. Being ignored tends to force them to be heard in other ways.

Taylor would agree with this. She has spent time and her own money replacing Confederate flags on the graves, not because she agrees with the politics of the Old South but because history is history, even with its ugly times. She points to how respectful people are of the graves on the other side of the road, but how careless they are in the haunted section. They ride their cars and ATVs over the overgrown graves and party at night and break bottles over the headstones. They litter where people are trying to find peace. "That doesn't happen in the other part."

The question remains: Are the ghost reacting to the living, or are the disrespectful people who use the cemetery somehow impacted by the negative energy of the cemetery?

And negative is how most people report the ghosts there. Toward the back, there were once two creepy pillars, probably memorials to the Pike family. These drew the attention of people looking for ghosts. It was said they marked the original entrance to the burial grounds, which is odd, considering they faced a citrus field and not a road. But urban legend said it was actually a gateway into another dimension. This allowed evil to come from all around into the town of Umatilla. Only one of the pillars remains today, but the stories survive. People hear growling in that part of the cemetery and have been hit or scratched. A man's voice is heard repeating that people need to leave. A woman is heard screaming, and women with long hair will have it pulled in that part of the grounds. It has become the place to go to get a good ghost photo.

"The whole place is scary," says Clara, who used to bike with her friends in high school to look for ghosts and challenge each other to go in alone.

The Pike headstone, which some believe acts as a gateway to a darker place.

"From the moment you walk near it, there are eyes on you. Think of a pretty girl walking by a bunch of guys on their coffee break. That's what it feels like. They are just looking you up and down. Ready to jump you. I'm not sure if you can understand that, but that's it. Checking you out and ready to attack."

Cars tend to break down in front of the cemetery, and flat tires occur as vehicles pass. It's a going joke in the town that the ghosts have to force people to stop and pay attention to them. Other entities among the headstones give

Could this tree be where the Woman in White sometimes looks for her children and plays with them?

the impression they do not want to be seen. There are rumors of a tall, dark figure that follows people but then disappears when people look around to get a better look. They can hear something run off, often to the back and across the field, but they can no longer see it. The snapping of branches or rustling of leaves is reported by many who go there to offer their respects.

The most infamous ghost there seems to be the most peaceful, which is odd, given the reputation of the place. A legend has developed about a young mother seen there. She is dressed all in white and wanders around, looking at the headstones near a large tree in the back section of the cemetery. She appears lost or as if she is looking for someone. People say she is a young mother looking for children who are buried nearby. At other times, she is seen with the children, playing near the tree and laughing with them. There are no graves near the tree that point to who the woman or the children might be, but in a place like Umatilla Cemetery, the story makes sense and is a better ghost to think about than what else might be there.

14

A Strange Thing Happened
in Astor

Elise is short. She's not so short that someone would point it out or make fun of her for it, but short enough that the higher shelves in the library are a bit out of her reach. Her office, like the two other offices in the temporary building (it has now been temporary for over ten years), reflects her personality, with tributes to horror movies and comics and Harry Potter. In the corner is a set of shelves that house little bits and pieces of the multiple programs the library hosts. A shelf with games for the kids is just a little too high for her. So, once, when she reached for the blue bucket she wanted, she knew there was a good chance she was not going to get it on the first try. Luckily, the game moved into her hand, courtesy of one of the several resident ghosts in the library.

"The blue bucket that's up there was pushed way back. I said, 'Hey, I can't reach it.' The next thing I know it's shoved into my hand."

When you hear the story of the haunted library she works in, what is unusual is not the helpful spirit she encountered that day, but the fact that this was just another moment for her. Activity has become so normal in the lives of the people who work there that it is no longer considered paranormal. The unexplained doesn't stop in the stacks. The library is located in Astor, Florida, and in a town like Astor, you get used to the ghosts or find another place to live. In this town, the supernatural and history dance with each other to create a complete picture of the town's landscape. If you run into someone who doesn't know a ghost story, chances are they don't live

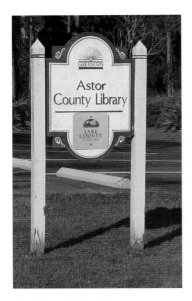

The Astor Public Library.

there. Everyone has one to tell or a version of one they heard from someone else, and experiences are passed off as the price of doing business and living on "Astor time." In a town rich with ghostly legends, the hiccups and flashes of the unexplained the residents go through are evidence that those old stories are true and proof that Astor is a place unlike most others.

The library is the center of the town in many ways. For a small rural collection, it consistently wins awards for its programming and events, as so many of the townspeople find their way there over the course of the week. If you don't know to take the turn off the main road to get to it, you'd miss it, but there are few residents who do not know where it is. Hidden off that road, the library acts as a pit stop for many children and teens living there but also a place where people get their news and town history.

And the history of the town, much like that of the library, is haunted. It was discovered in 1562 by a French Huguenot, Admiral Jean Ribaut, and it did not take long for others to arrive and establish a settlement. The residents made friends with the Timucua tribe in the area, who warned them to stay away from the east side of the river, now known as the St. Johns. From the start, people were told there was something dark about the water and the forest beyond it. When the Spanish arrived a few years later, they wiped out the French and established a monastery, San Juan del Puerto. The Timucua, who had lived in peace with the Huguenots, reacted by killing everyone in the monastery and burning it down. The head abbot was brought to the center of town, tortured and hanged. His body was to be left hanging, but during the night a weird fog rolled into town, and the dead monk began wandering around, looking for those who had killed him. Most ran, but the chief decided to confront the ghost. The next morning, he was found dead from no visible cause. Since that night, the monk walks the streets of Astor at foggy times under the cover of darkness.

People have reported him all over the town, or at least attribute the large shadowy figure they see to the man. Astor, like so many places near the Ocala, has its own Dark Man. Lists of haunted places in Florida include

The librarian's work area in the Astor Public Library where several different ghosts have been known to play with things.

sightings of the man on Gobbler Road or in the Gobbler Road Campsite. They report that he taps on windows or bangs on doors. On the road, people report seeing him wander, and they often drive straight through him. Tara recalls seeing him one night in 2005. "It was late. My husband was drunk, but I was stone sober. He was there, just walking on the edge of the road. A normal person, right? No. I moved my car to the middle of the road so it wouldn't scare him. I passed him, and it was not human. It was shaped like a tall man, but there was no face and no, like, body parts." She says her husband never saw him, and an odd feeling made her shake the rest of the way home.

This man is said by some to be Okie, who may or may not be a ghost. That all depends on whether you believe a man can live to be over 150 years old and disappear at will. His real name was Oklawahumpka, the last chief of a forgotten tribe that has changed names over the years. He was a fierce warrior who refused to surrender to settlers and explorers and was said to be unable to be killed. Several people tried over the years, and an alligator bit off one of his toes when he was a child, creating a distinct, four-toed footprint still seen throughout Astor. He eventually realized he could no longer actively fight with his people gone, so he ripped his totem (with a war hawk on the top) and moved to what is now Morrison Island to retire. It is written that in the late 1800s, several expeditions left to try to tame the island and investigate odd reports of monsters and dragons seen from the other side of the water. No one ever returned, and each party disappeared into the darkness with only the scream of a hawk being heard.

This gave rise to a legend people have experienced time and time again on the banks of Morrison Island. If you stand on the other side (the best view is from the docks of the Jungle Den RV Park), you can see Okie come out of the trees, look around to make sure everything is okay and retreat back into the darkness. Jennifer has seen him several times and swears the figure she sees is real but entirely human. "At 11:30 you can see an old Indian walk out from the island out to the water. I heard about it, but never believed. Then I went there with some girlfriends and watched it. They said they saw him before that night too."

Her boyfriend Charlie even went with her one night, certain that the story was nothing but town spookiness. "She took me out there. I didn't want to leave because I felt something. Something was out there. I was just watching it. It was like it was there and not. And I was just watching it." Both give the same description of a dark statue of a man with no features that walks with a stiff, almost majestic stride. One couple even saw it walk down into the water one night, accompanied by a mysterious splash. They then saw nothing but a head skimming the surface of the water.

Then there is the story of the phantom train whistle heard on Railroad Grading Road. While no one really knows the story behind what they hear, for years it has been passed down and shared. "Everybody knows about it," says Elise, "but we can't find anything out about it. There's no history about

Morrison Island, where Okie is said to roam.

where it was or when it happened, but we all believe it did. It's mentioned a few places, but only that there was a train wreck. That's all we found." At a nearby train stop, harvested grapes were picked up in the town and loaded to be carried away and made into wine. On the same trains was a steerage section that moved people along the rail. According to the lore, a horrible train wreck took the lives of at least a dozen people. If you travel down Railroad Grading at night, you can often hear a train whistle coming from the trees. At times, witnesses have also heard the screams of the people who lost their lives in the accident. Some people have even spotted ghost lights along with the sounds.

While these stories tend to be town legends, for Elise and the other librarians, Jonathan and Margee, what happens in the library is much more personal, with an ever-changing cast of characters.

"We see a man in the windows," says Elise. "We walk to the front of the building, and you can see him in one of the chairs in Jonathan's office." Jonathan has seen the man, too, and feels he's attracted to the odd and antique items Jonathan likes to store there. Something has been known to play with his old-fashioned clock, because the activity began when he brought it in. The ghost also enjoys playing with the dolls the staff bring in and display on the chairs. The ghost may also be the one that plays with their coffee machine and likes to smoke cigars in that part of the library in the afternoon. A dark figure has been seen near the area where Triston, Elise's son, and another worker at the library often sit. "I was here alone and came back through the hallway, and he was sitting where Triston sits," says Jonathan, who describes the man as having dark hair but cannot offer more of a description. "I'm not sure if it's embedded emotions or something, but it just seemed too solid to be that. I turned back around, and he wasn't there."

Elise adds to his story. "I was sitting here last week. It's just a strong, strong smell. We smelled it in the morning while we were having our coffee. We hadn't gotten any new books in, so there was nothing coming from the books. It was definitely a sweet tobacco scent."

"There are two kids who run around here too; a little boy and a little girl. I've seen the little girl. You can see her running up and down from the kid's section to the back and all around. She has a little yellow dress with a little lace on the bottom, and little Mary Janes. Little, short-cropped, bobbed dark hair." Elise believes this little girl makes people sick when they come back toward the bathrooms and has even visited her there, although it might be an older version of the same girl. "I am in the lady's room and the door

Railroad Grading Road, home to a phantom train and a mysterious Dark Man.

does not open. I see a skirt and woman's ballet shoes go past my stall. It was like a '60s style patchwork skirt that's coming back right now. It was down to the ankles. I don't hear anything in the other stall. I get out and look around. There are a few guys out here and three girls. They're all in jeans and sneakers, no ballet shoes. I went back and looked around, and no one was in there."

Both ghost children like to have their way in the place, although usually when no one is there but the staff. "There are these rocker chairs in the teen section," says Elise. "One day, I was putting up books, and I thought I saw her sitting there. Then I was putting away books and I felt a little hand, like a child's hand, come around and grab mine. Just stand there and hold my hand for a second. I'll see a little arm going flying down the aisle, and I'll say, 'Don't run.'" Margee has set up the CD player to use for a kid's program, only to have it go off by itself or stop working when she needed it to.

Margee, who has had multiple experiences at her house as well, thinks one of the ghost children wanted their Halloween candy one year. "I'm sitting in my office and there's this bag of candy. Out of nowhere, I hear the bag rustling. I thought it was Triston getting into the candy, so I didn't pay attention. But it just kept going. I looked around the corner and there was nobody there. But the rustling was still going on. I went over and picked up the bag, and I could still hear the candy wrappers moving in the bag. I brought Elise in and we both sat here and listened. Something hit the bottom of my hand and I freaked. It still gives me chills. I said, 'I am taking this bag outside,' because I thought something was in it. I closed it and walked out the front door, and I kept hearing the rattling. I dumped the candy on the cement. I didn't see anything moving. It was like the lemon drops were the ones they wanted. I threw them all in the bushes."

You would think all of these ghosts running around the place would make all of this normal for the library workers, but a few years ago, even they were disturbed by another presence that started to make itself known. A man began working there that did not mix well with the vibe of the other librarians, although they do not like to get into the details. With him seemed to come a dark presence that enjoyed walking back and forth in the nonfiction section. He was not a man as much as a short, gray, shadow-like figure with a football-shaped head. All of the employees report having felt a chill when in that area during the time the man worked there. They would be working in other parts of the library and look down toward the section and see the spirit wrap its hands around the shelves with almost alien-like fingers and pop out from behind that stack, as if spying on them before drawing back quickly.

Once, Jonathan was in the aisle getting a book that had been placed on hold. He was thinking about the book he was considering writing on the history of Astor and thinking about a specific book he wanted to use for research. He continued down the aisle, and the exact book he had been thinking about, *The History of Astor on the St. John's, Astor Park, and the Surrounding Area*, fell off the shelf and onto the floor behind him. Soon after, the other man quit working at the library, and the nonfiction entity seemed to go with him, making the other ghosts there more playful than spooky again.

The stacks in the Astor Public Library where the ghostly children are seen.

Jonathan feels the ghost in the nonfiction section was trying to tell him to keep working and publish the book, something that resonates with him regarding many of the odd things he experiences there. He believes the library employees are receiving messages, most of which are merely to try to uncover the lost history of the town. All of them have their own theories of what might be in the library and what it all means—not that anything they research can confirm what they think. The grounds where the library stands was swamp, filled in to make a space for the temporary library and the park next door. There is no history of the land they can find. There have been murders nearby in the past, as well as a suicide just down the road and the mysterious death of the first drawbridge worker at the border of Astor and Deland, but nothing solid. Instead, it feels more like the library is as much a stopover and rest area for the dead as much as it is a facility for the living.

Soon, the staff and the books and the energy will be moved into a new building, and the temporary will become permanent. The library will not be in the same location, and the staff is left wondering if the ghosts will come along with them. What they have experienced may become just another piece of the puzzle of the weird experiences that occur while spending one's days living on Astor time—another town myth told by people when they get together to tell haunted legends and share experiences. Margee and Elise will miss the ghosts if they don't come along, but they also know that in a town like Astor, there's always another ghost story waiting to be spread.

BIBLIOGRAPHY

Allen, Rick. "As the Old OCT Building Faces Likely Demolition, Former Inhabitants Say Thanks for the Memories." *Ocala Star-Banner*, June 8, 2016.

———. "Meet the Magician Who Built—and Perhaps Haunted—the Old Ocala Civic Theatre." *Ocala Star-Banner*, June 9, 2016.

Ashley, Taylor. "Ghosts of Lilian Place Ready to Entertain." *Daytona Beach News-Journal*, October 25, 2012.

BackPackerVerse. "Devilish Ghosts Grasp for the Living at Haunted Astor Car Camping Site." November 2017. https://backpackerverse.com.

———. "Flesh-Ripping Ghost Family Terrorizes Cars on This Florida Road." November 2020. https://backpackerverse.com.

———. "These 8 Urban Legends in Florida Will Keep You Awake at Night." November 2020. https://backpackerverse.com.

Balzano, Christopher. *Haunted Florida Love Stories*. Charleston, SC: The History Press, 2019.

Bench, Marnie. "Osteen Cemetery in Osteen, Florida." The Grave Girl. February 17, 2017. http://www.thegravegirl.com.

Carlson, Charles. *Weird Florida*. New York: Sterling Publishing, 2005.

Charley Project. "Nancy Elaine Leichner." June 7, 2020. https://charleyproject.org.

Dummire, Dana E. "For Whom the Bell Tolls (atop Hulley Tower)." *Stetson Reporter*, February 17, 1973.

Fernandez, Frank. "New Orange Avenue Bridge Gets Early Visitor…on the Top Arch." *Daytona Beach News-Journal*, August 6, 2020.

Goudsward, David. *Horror Guide to Florida: A Literary Travel Guide* (Horror Guides Book 2). Cincinnati, OH: Post Mortem Press, 2015.

Haunted Places. "Pine Ridge High School." June 7, 2020. https://www.hauntedplaces.org.

Jenkins, Greg. *Florida's Ghostly Legends and Haunted Folklore: South and Central Florida*. Sarasota, FL: Pineapple Publishing, 2013.

Johnson, Pat. "The Oviedo Lights: Can It Kill." *FuTUre*, October 10, 1969.

Lisk, Nettie. "Legends of Silver Springs." *Ocala Evening Star*, June 12, 1907.

Long, Nancy Zrinyi. *Ghosts of Lilian Place: True Accounts of Strange Events at the 1884 House*. Columbia, SC: CreateSpace, 2019.

Mimna, Robin. "Deltona's Misplaced History: The Lost Community of Saulsville." Medium, June 7, 2020. https://medium.com.

Muncy, Mark. *Freaky Florida*. Charleston, SC: The History Press, 2018.

Nelson, William. "Tampa's Stikini Witches." Florida Folklore, November 8, 2012. http://floridafolk.blogspot.com.

Paranormal Ghost Society. "Umatilla Cemetery." Paranormal Ghost Society, June 7, 2020. http://paranormalghostsociety.org.

Schlenker, Dave. "Morris and Memories at the Old OCT." *Ocala Star-Banner*, June 2, 2016.

Smith, Dusty. *Haunted DeLand and the Ghosts of West Volusia County*. Charleston, SC: The History Press, 2008.

Steele, W.S. "Last Command: The Dade Massacre." *Journal of the Historical Association of Southern Florida* 46 (1986): 5–19.

Walls, Kathleen. *Finding Florida's Phantoms*. Toronto, ON: Global Authors Publications, 2004.

Wass de Czege, Albert. *The History of Astor on the St. John's, Astor Park, and the Surrounding Area*. Astor, FL: Danubian Press, 1982.

ABOUT THE AUTHOR

Christopher Balzano is a writer, researcher, folklorist and current host of the podcast *Tripping on Legends*. He has been documenting the unexplained since 1994 and has been a figure in the paranormal world through his books, articles and work as the director of Massachusetts Paranormal Crossroads and now Tripping on Legends.

Balzano is the author of several books about regional hauntings, *Dark Woods: Cults Crime and the Paranormal in the Freetown State Forest* and *Ghosts of the Bridgewater Triangle*; the collections of true ghost stories *Ghostly Adventures* and *Haunted Objects: Stories of Ghosts on Your Shelf*; and the how-to paranormal books *Picture Yourself Ghost Hunting* and *Picture Yourself Capturing Ghosts on Film*. He is also the author of *Haunted Florida Love Stories* (The History Press), a journey through the ghostly legends of the state that all have love as part of their backstory.

He has been a contributor to Jeff Belanger's *Encyclopedia of Haunted Places* and *Weird Massachusetts* and was one of the writers behind *Weird Hauntings*. He has appeared in more than two dozen other books, often called in to offer insights into the paranormal or perspective on a certain case.

He has appeared on radio stations across the country and via the internet and has been called on by television shows to comment on ghosts and urban legends, including the British television series *Conversations with a Serial Killer*. He has been a guest on *Coast to Coast AM* and been asked in as a consultant on television shows like *Paranormal State* and *Ghost Adventures*. He formerly ran the Paranormal News at Ghostvillage and headed up Ghostvillage for Kids.